THE
BLOCK PLAN
PRESCHOOL

PARENT HANDBOOK

Katy Harder

FAMILIES AT
PLAY

COPYRIGHT

ALL RIGHTS RESERVED

DISCLAIMERS

The publisher and the author cannot be held responsible for injury, mishap, or damages incurred during the use of or because of the information or activities in this book. The author recommends appropriate and reasonable supervision at all times based on the age and capability of each child.

Many of the designations used by manufacturers and sellers to distinguish their products are claimed as trademarks. Where those designations appear in this book and the author was aware of a trademark claim, the designations have been printed in initial capital letters (i.e., Reeboks).

All personal names referenced in the text have been changed to protect privacy.

BULK PURCHASE

Families at Play books are available at special discount when purchased in bulk. Special editions or book excerpts also can be created to specification. For more information contact us at katy@blockplanpreschool.com or at the address or phone number on this page.

DEDICATION

To my mom, Cathy, and husband, Ron, thank you for holding my hands and always having faith. I love you both so much!

ACKNOWLEDGEMENTS

No mom is an island, I certainly am not, and I'm grateful to the many people who have contributed directly and indirectly to this project over the years. Thank you to family, friends and neighbors surrounding me in life who are all supportive, encouraging, interesting, intelligent, kind, fun and generous people. Thank you to everyone who backed this project on Kickstarter, I so appreciate your faith in me and The Block Plan Preschool!

To Keri Lysaght, thank you for giving me a chance, you have been in my heart and on my mind ever since that first interview. Thank you to those who have taught me, inspired me, hired me, and helped me become a better teacher: Alice Hulen, Mary Avila, Earlene Jones, Veronica Lewis, Cyrus Weinberger, Sarah Pekala, David Secunda, Kyle Littman and Janelle Langetieg.

Thank you to Cathlin Jones, Adam York, Courtney Brinks and Tessa Taggart, the first parents to try out my curriculum with their children. Whether you meant to or not, you provided me abundant inspiration, challenge, encouragement, perspective, and accountability to deadlines along the way, thank you!

Thank you to Carrie Aitkenhead, Melissa Bernstein and everyone else at Melissa and Doug who is working on the Take Back Childhood movement! Thank you for your support of me, my curriculum project and my family as we try to protect the joys and freedoms of childhood for our children. I am inspired, honored and motivated by our partnership!

To my family, thank you for your constant and unwavering support and encouragement. To my mom and editor, Cathy Stypula, thank you for teaching me that if anyone can do it I can do it, and for passing on your love of books! To my dad, Gary Stypula, thank you for encouraging me to live my best life and for doing all those experiments with us as kids. To my brother and sister-in-law, Tommy and Lorena Stypula, thank you for reminding me how much fun it is to do things my own way.

To my husband, Ron, thank you for working so hard at what you do so that I can do this. Babe, you make everything possible! Thank you for always being my sounding board and encouraging companion. To my son, Trevor, thank you for bringing so much light to my life and for giving me so many ideas. To our new baby Kaia, we can't wait to share the fun with you too! I love you all so much!

CONTENTS

INTRODUCTION

"Today families are caught in a paradox. We're parenting during a time when scientists increasingly tell us that free play is vital to the health of our kids, yet schools and policies are pushing us in the opposite direction - in an agitated rush toward early academics. The gap between what we know about young children and what we do with young children is widening every year."

– Heather Shumaker, *It's OK Not to Share*

"We know that the first five years have so much to do with how the next 80 turn out."

– William H. Gates, Sr., Co-chair of the Bill and Melinda Gates Foundation

I t is my opinion that we have abundant research and resources today that describe what we should not do as parents, but fewer resources that give us tools describing what we should do. This book is a response to the information that tells us to provide free play and an unstructured life for our children by giving us the tools to actually do that. It isn't right to leave our child completely to his own devices, but nor is it right to push him academically at such a young age. The Block Plan Preschool is a prescription for the problems that ail modern families and the challenges we currently face as parents.

The Block Plan Preschool method of kindergarten preparation has more to do with creating a happy learner, creative thinker and confident human being than with drilling children on actual academic knowledge. In the process of creating an inspired learner you will see that your child will acquire quite a bit of knowledge, but it will be at an age-appropriate pace and according to her interests. As you may have already discovered, The Block Plan Preschool is a tool to invite more free play and less structure into your child's life while still offering rich, inspiring experiences to engage her active brain.

Research has told us for years that play is so important for kids' health and brain development, but our social culture is making it more and more difficult for parents to bow out of an overscheduled method of parenting. The Block Plan Preschool should make it easy for you to do this by providing flexible learning experiences you can use to educate your child at home so that you can be confident that he knows all he needs to know before beginning school. You do not need to depend on or invest in external programs to achieve a level of readiness for your child, you just need time, energy and the organized approach provided in this book.

As you work your way through the curriculum with your family, I hope you will remember that when you're not doing Block Plan Preschool activities, you can and should provide a lot of free play and exploration time for your young child. As David Elkind writes in *Miseducation: Preschoolers at Risk*,

> Young children are not just sitting twiddling their thumbs, waiting for their parents to teach them to read and do math. They are expending a vast amount of time and effort in exploring and understanding their immediate world. Healthy education supports and encourages this spontaneous learning.

At the same time Elkind also writes, "You can never miseducate children by responding appropriately to their demands for information."

This is the balance we strive for: to create a world for our children that gives them time, support and freedom to work through the task of making sense of this complicated world; to equip them to be as autonomous as is appropriate; and to provide information and learning opportunities as they desire. The Block Plan Preschool is the best way I know how to find that balance of free play and learning opportunities and I hope it helps you do the same for your young children. You are doing a good thing by striving for the right balance in your child's life and I wish you the best as you travel this important educational journey together.

Welcoming Free Play

1. Make literacy joyful
2. Go outside
3. Choose open-ended toys
4. Offer space
5. Cut structured activities
6. Look for a play-based preschool
7. Slow down

(Excerpt from *It's OK Not to Share* by Heather Shumaker)

"When a child shows up for school and is not physically or mentally ready to learn, he or she never catches up."

– C. Everett Koop, Former Surgeon General Of the United States

After years of teaching preschool, my last position before becoming a stay-at-home mom was in a kindergarten classroom in a public elementary school. One of my responsibilities was testing children in literacy and math skills so that teachers could place the students in the correct ability groups. In one class I tested two different children, Violet and Sean. They had been in the same preschool class at the same public school, which was designed to feed into the kindergarten class they were in now. Both the preschool teacher and the kindergarten teacher were excellent educators and had a great working relationship with each other. There was no reason to suspect that either child would be behind upon entering kindergarten, but their test scores told a different story, and they were placed in opposite ability groups in both literacy and math.

Why did this happen? The disparity did not appear to be only based on intelligence or ability to focus, nor was it formal educational background. It did not seem to have to do with temperament or personality as the two children had comparable social skills and classroom behaviors. I had an opportunity to get to know both families as the year progressed and there did not appear to be a disparity in socioeconomic status. The only difference I could detect that would lead to such a difference in knowledge was in the respective families' approaches to education.

Sean had two younger brothers and his mother was a former professor at a university. She was now a stay-at-home mom and generally gave off an air of always having enough time for whatever needed to happen. Of course sometimes she was late or in a rush, but most of the time she would stay after school while her boys played on the playground and chat with me about how the school day went. I would offer details such as, "We worked on sight words today and Sean really did well." She would often respond with something such as, "Great! We've been practicing those." Sean scored very well at the beginning of the year in both literacy and math, he seemed comfortable reciting his knowledge and quietly confident. He did not seem flustered by the testing process and would thoughtfully and carefully respond to all questions. This trend continued throughout the school year, Sean was a lovely child, enjoyed school and felt sure of himself even as new challenges were presented.

Violet's mom was also a stay-at-home parent and walked to school for drop-off and pick-up each day. She was often late, however, and generally gave off a busy, hurried and harried air. Most days I would wait with Violet outside while the other children were picked up and taken home, which was a source of minor embarrassment for her. More concerning than this, however, is that I didn't get the sense that Violet was practicing or learning much at home. She did not score well on the initial tests in literacy and math, and she was very quiet during the process and felt embarrassed not to know the answers. By the end of the first test she wasn't even responding verbally when I asked, "Do you know what sound this letter makes?" She would just look at me with a small grimace and we would continue. I reassured her many times during testing to try to help her feel better, but I felt my efforts only made minimal difference. She knew that because I was asking the questions they contained information she should know and felt badly that she did not. This trend continued throughout the year as Violet was very quiet in school and seemed unsure of herself in general. She was a lovely child and had no reason to feel self-conscious except I'm sure she knew she was behind, and I don't think that feeling ever left her.

The preparation, knowledge and skills with which your child enters kindergarten are instrumental in forming his or her self-image.

This story helps us in two ways. For one, it shows how parents can impact a child's education from the earliest stages. It is important that you practice and teach your child at home because formal schooling, even the best programs, won't be enough to adequately challenge and prepare your child for a lifetime of engaged learning. Second, it demonstrates how the preparation, knowledge and skills with which your child enters kindergarten are instrumental in forming his or her self-image. At about five years old children become much more aware of how they fit into groups socially. They move into Piaget's stage of play called "cooperative play," meaning they are able to play group games with rules such as tag and duck-duck-goose more effectively (Santrock, 2007; Ginsburg, 1988). (Up until this age those types of games are usually a big group of kids all running around together in more of a state of chaos!)

At this kindergarten-age stage in development children begin to care about others' opinions of them, show a desire for friendships and demonstrate awareness of social dynamics for the first time (Santrock, 2007). This is an important stage in your child's formation of identity and is a wonderful opportunity for you to instill a sense of confidence that will last for many years to come. It is unfortunate to see a child who has the ability and interest to learn and succeed, but doesn't have the tools to do so.

The purpose of most preschools is to prepare children to be in school, not to provide them with all the knowledge they need to succeed. This is because schools simply do not have enough time to teach children individually and instead mostly focus on group lessons. Many preschools are wonderful and many teachers are wonderful, but as parents we must correctly understand the purpose of formal preschools as we make an educational plan for our children. In formal preschool, you can expect that children will learn skills such as how to go on a field trip, go to the bathroom at a scheduled bathroom break, play cooperatively on the playground, sit quietly at circle time, and join in songs and games. These are important social skills, but do not create a foundation of academic knowledge for your child.

I once had a student named Ethan in my two-day preschool class, meaning the students come to school for three hours per day, twice a week. Ethan was four years old, loved school and played well with other children, but did not have much academic knowledge. One day he was sitting in front of a counting poster on the classroom wall while we were getting ready for snack time. I went over and counted with him while he pointed to items and numbers on the poster, he was so happy! Every day he would ask me to count with him and I got the sense no one had ever done this with him before. Because I was teaching an entire class, however, I only had a few minutes to spend with Ethan individually and therefore couldn't make much progress on math skills throughout the year. I told his parents this, but I don't think they made much effort to practice with him at home. Ethan is an example of a child who has the interest and ability, but not the resources to learn.

The Block Plan Preschool will give you the tools and guidance to provide your child a great education that will help them feel confident no matter what kindergarten throws at them. Your child will learn literacy, math, science, art, music, and motor skills that will create a strong base of knowledge. Your child will learn to think through problems, assess risk and keep himself safe, behave cooperatively and generously, and develop a sense of confidence and self-respect that will be a foundation to build upon for the rest of his life. This is the purpose of The Block Plan Preschool, to help you create a strong and lasting foundation of knowledge, connectedness and confidence so that your child can enter kindergarten with a strong sense of self. Do it in the way that works best for you, love your child and give her what you can. We're here to help.

Your child will develop a sense of confidence and self-respect.

THE BLOCK PLAN PRESCHOOL PHILOSOPHY

"Early childhood is a very important period of life. It is a period when children learn an enormous amount about the everyday world. It is also the time during which young children acquire lifelong attitudes toward themselves, toward others, and toward learning. But it is not the time for formal academic instruction."

– David Elkind,
Miseducation: Preschoolers at Risk

I believe that every parent can and should be able to teach preschool lessons at home to his or her own child affordably and effectively. Research and the resulting opinions of psychologists and child development professionals support the philosophy accepted by most educators that parents' engagement and influence is an integral part of a child's educational life (Maxwell and Clifford, 2004). The Block Plan Preschool curriculum is based on the following four philosophies about young children.

I. Young children need consistency and calm in order to advance academically.

Have you ever transplanted a tree? For the first year after transplant the tree "sleeps" and hardly grows at all, the second year the tree "creeps" and the third year it finally "leaps" and you can see significant new growth. When you move a tree it takes time and energy for the tree to adjust to new soil, moisture and weather conditions, and it must regrow and spread its trimmed roots. After a move, the tree must do all this before making any forward progress.

Children are much the same way in that they cannot learn, grow and thrive if their energy is constantly being diverted to adjusting to new environments. David Elkind describes this as "change overload" in his book *The Hurried Child* where he writes,

> Now consider Peter, a boy four years old. Both his mother and father work and they have enrolled him in a full-day private nursery. In addition, because both parents have to leave home early, they have arranged to leave Peter with a neighbor, who will prepare him for the car pool person, who will take him to school before nine o'clock. After school, the car pool person drops him off at the neighbor's house again until his parents come to pick him up after work. By the time he gets home, Peter has been out of the house for almost twelve

hours and has adapted to a number of different places (neighbor's house, car, school) and a number of different people (neighbor, car pool person, teachers).

This is a lot of adaptation for a four-year-old, and he has had to call upon his energy reserves in order to cope. Is it really surprising that his teachers complain that he is whining and fussy, that he does not seem interested in playing with the other children, and that he sometimes sits quietly staring into space while touching two blocks together, back and forth, back and forth? Peter is clearly at the limit of his energy reserves. He suffers from change overload.

In this description Peter has had to use all his brain power to cope with changing environments and has nothing left for growth and learning. The possibility of change overload does not necessarily mean that day care or organized preschool is bad for kids. On the contrary, social environments in quality programs are good for kids, but what they learn in those programs are primarily social lessons such as how to play with others and how to be part of a group. In order for your child to learn new academic concepts, you need to provide a familiar, calm, comfortable, quiet environment that is devoid of stress so that all the child's brain power can be used for learning.

2. Young children need to connect abstract academic concepts with concrete experiences in order to learn effectively.

Experiential learning is an effective approach to education for all people, but I believe it is especially useful and important for young children who require experimentation to learn about themselves, their world and their own capabilities. In my first preschool class I had a boy who seemed disorderly compared to the other children. I came home and told my husband about the things this child was doing on the playground such as kicking a ball as hard as he could in a confined area. My husband is a physical therapist and told me he was probably learning about force and his own physical abilities through this experimentation. I had never thought of it that way as my perspective came from a goal of maintaining order and safety for the other children who were getting hit by the flying ball. Upon learning that he was trying to figure out how strong he was, how much force it takes to move the ball, how far he can make it go and how to move his body to create a desired result, I was able to create other activities for him that would better protect the other children while satisfying his need to experiment in this way. There was no other way for this child to learn these lessons other that trying it out. Nothing I could have described verbally or visually could have helped him learn what he was seeking, only a concrete experience could teach him these scientific and physical lessons. As Patty Born Selly writes in *Early Childhood Activities for a Greener Earth*, "For an adult to give a correct or scientific explanation *without connecting to the child's real life experience* would be abstract and virtually meaningless."

Maria Montessori describes an event useful to our understanding in her landmark work *The Montessori Method*, writing:

> One day, the children had gathered themselves, laughing and talking, into a circle about a basin of water containing some float toys. We had in the school a little boy barely two and a half years old. He had been left outside the circle, alone, and it was easy to see that he was filled with intense curiosity. I watched him from a distance with great interest; he first drew near to the other children and tried to force his way among them, but he was not strong enough to do this, and he then stood looking about him. The expression of thought on his little face was intensely interesting. I wish that I had had a camera so that I might have photographed him. His eye lighted upon a little chair, and evidently he made up his mind to place it behind the group of children and then to climb up on it. He began to move toward the chair, his face illuminated with hope, but at that moment the teacher seized him brutally (or, perhaps, she would have said, gently) in her arms, and lifting him up above the heads of the other children showed him the basin of water, saying, 'Come, poor little one, you shall see too!'

"The expression of joy, anxiety and hope...faded from his face and left on it the stupid expression of the child who knows that others will act for him."

Undoubtedly the child, seeing the floating toys, did not experience the joy that he was about to feel through conquering the obstacle with his own force. The sight of those objects could be of no advantage to him, while his intelligent efforts would have developed his inner powers. The teacher hindered the child, in this case, from educating himself, without giving him any compensating good in return. The little fellow had been about to feel himself a conqueror, and he found himself held within two imprisoning arms, impotent. The expression of joy, anxiety, and hope, which had interested me so much faded from his face and left on it the stupid expression of the child who knows that others will act for him.

You are in a unique position of being able to guide your child into the type of learner you want her to be. Ideally, we want our children to be able to follow directions, but mostly we want them to feel they can try things out on their own in order to learn what we are trying to teach them. Children need to be able to experiment and explore how things work in order to learn effectively. They need to be allowed to move, touch, and make noise while learning even the most academic of concepts such as literacy and math skills in order to engage the appropriate parts of their brains.

In addition to concrete, kinesthetic experiences, children need concrete objects and relationships presented to them in order to process abstract concepts. Psychologists have long understood what they call the "relational shift" in the brain that happens for children sometime after six years of age and before 12 years old. During this time, the brain changes from understanding information thematically to understanding information based on other relationships. For example, in their paper titled "Two Forces in the Development of Relational Similarity," Gentner and Ratterman et al. describe the shift writing:

> Young infants tend to respond to overall (literal) similarity and identity between scenes, such as the similarity between a red ball rolling and another red ball rolling. The earliest partial matches are based on *object similarity*: direct resemblances between objects, such as the similarity between a round red ball and a round red apple. With increasing knowledge, children come to make single-attribute matches such as the similarity between a red ball and a red car, and finally, *relational similarity* matches, such as the similarity between a ball *rolling on* a table and a toy car *rolling on* the floor. For example, when asked to interpret metaphors like *A tape recorder is like a camera*, 6-year-olds produced object-based interpretations such as *Both are metal and black*, whereas 9-year-olds and adults focused chiefly on common relational structure (e.g., *Both can record something for later*; Gentner 1988).

The Block Plan Preschool organizes lessons thematically, because that is how children think during early childhood years. By creating experiential and experimental lessons to engage young children's brains and bodies and then organizing the lessons into monthly themes we are maximizing the potential for young children to absorb information. We are also creating confident, engaged learners with a solid background of experiences and knowledge that will inform their future approaches to learning when they enter school.

3. Young children need time, materials and experiences that help them develop senses of curiosity, initiative, exploration and autonomy both alone and with a parent.

Somewhere along the line it seems that we started believing as a society that education takes place outside the home. While there are many camps, lessons, schools and classes that can add value to your child's life, these do not need to be and probably shouldn't be the backbone of her early experiences. Relationship with parents is a crucial part of your child's learning, both in her personality development and in her actual academic progress. In *The Hurried Child* David Elkind writes,

> A child's sense of initiative, curiosity, and exploration is strengthened when parents take time to answer the child's questions, when they provide materials and opportunities for exploration and discovery, and when they do not get un-

duly upset by the resulting clutter and debris... Young children need time to explore and investigate in a responsive environment if they are to acquire a sense of initiative stronger than a sense of guilt. When preschoolers are hurried from one caregiver to another, or from one lesson to another, they may be deprived of the opportunity to explore their environment freely. Likewise, if parents are too busy or too tired to answer the child's questions, the child may feel guilty about asking them. When the child's efforts at initiative are blocked or shot down, the child's sense of guilt will be the predominant orientation acquired at this stage. An overwhelming sense of guilt established in early childhood may result in a lifelong orientation of tentativeness and fearfulness about initiating new projects.

As you can see from this passage no matter what activities in which you enroll your child outside the home, the environment you establish at home as a parent will always be the greatest influencer in his learning. A child who is afraid to initiate exploration and experimentation cannot be a creative and critical thinker. The Block Plan Preschool is a resource that will help you establish an environment and relationships in your home that will support learning from the beginning of your child's life.

"These tools and programs are heavily marketed, and many parents have grown to believe that they are a requirement of good parenting."

So why do so many parents do it? Why do we enroll our kids in so many programs outside the home if we know that they need calm time and they need time with us? A study published in *Pediatrics* titled, "The Importance of Play in Promoting Parent-Child Bonds," describes a theory of why this happens:

Specialized gyms and enrichment programs designed for children exist in many communities, and there is an abundance of after-school enrichment activities. These tools and programs are heavily marketed, and many parents have grown to believe that they are a requirement of good parenting and a necessity for appropriate development. As a result, much of parent-child time is spent arranging special activities or transporting children between those activities. In addition to time, considerable family financial resources are being invested to ensure that the children have what are marketed as the 'very best' opportunities... Many parents seem to feel as though they are running on a treadmill to keep up yet dare not slow their pace for fear their children will fall behind. In addition, some worry they will not be acting as proper parents if they do not participate in this hurried lifestyle.

I first started feeling this way when my son was eighteen months old and a well-meaning neighbor asked if I had gotten him on the waiting list for the "best preschool in town" yet. My response was to write The Block Plan Preschool curriculum. I didn't want to participate in that child-achievement culture, so I created an alternate plan that would bring my family closer together instead of pushing us apart in different directions and into different activities outside the home. I hope it does the same for your family and gives you permission and tools to step off the treadmill.

The Block Plan Preschool curriculum will build you up as a parent, help reduce clutter of books and toys in your home, inspire curiosity in your child, engage your whole family in the early learning process and give you the tools to structure your family's life the way you want it to be without being beholden to any busy or expensive external schedules. You can provide early learning experiences through the activities you probably already do with your kids, such as reading books, visiting the zoo, painting, and exploring in the backyard. The Block Plan Preschool curriculum will organize those activities into a thematic structure that makes sense to your child's developing brain and builds on what is happening seasonally in his world. This will help you and your child get the most out of the things you do together, because as we have learned, there is no one in your young child's life more important than you, the parent.

4. Young children need to explore academic concepts at their own pace and according to their own interests.

I think of cultivating a well-rounded learner the same way you would think of cultivating a healthy eater (both are important goals for any child). Just because your child really likes Pop-Tarts, for example, doesn't mean you should give them only Pop-Tarts (low nutritional value, high fun factor), but nor does it mean you should never give them Pop-Tarts. On the flip side, just because your child doesn't like carrots at first doesn't mean you shouldn't keep putting them on the plate. To cultivate a healthy eater you need to include enjoyment and nutrition into the repertoire so that your child develops a healthy and happy relationship with food and eating. As it is with academics (called "choice learning"), if your child loves something fun go with it! And keep offering the healthy thing you hope they will be interested in until someday they are.

The first time we took my son to The Butterfly Pavilion, which is a popular invertebrate exhibit near our home, he didn't like any of the insects, beetles, scorpions, spiders or even the butterflies. He wasn't interested and didn't want to be around them. Instead of accepting that he just doesn't like that place, however, we took him there again after completing the insect unit in The Block Plan Preschool. This time he loved it! He spent several minutes in each section of the exhibit exclaiming things like, "Look Mom! It's a beetle!" He watched the critters he had read about in his books with fascination and bravely approached the ones that scared him. Child development professionals generally recommend offering a food to your child 10 times before accepting that he may not like it and The Block Plan Preschool subscribes to the same philosophy for educational activities. Just because your child doesn't like it today, doesn't mean she won't be interested at another time.

Of course, pushing your child too hard is not a good idea either. In *The Trouble with Perfect*, the authors write,

> When parents begin to push, they risk damaging the secure attachment that cushions children as they make their way through the world. Children whose parents are focused primarily on outcome—making the honor roll, making the team, making the college —learn, explicitly or implicitly, that if they don't hold up their end of the bargain, their parents will love them less. This scenario is grossly simplified, of course. But there is evidence that children who are pressured, or who have learned to focus only on goals, are less creative, spontaneous, and eager to experiment. They tend to be anxious and inhibited... To develop a strong sense of self, children must feel free to fail. This is a critical component of any achievement... Children become anxious when they are pressured into achieving goals rather than concentrating on the process of an activity. They are more likely to give up, or find themselves unable to do their best, than their unpressured peers.

Knowing how hard to push a child is a challenge for all educators, especially with young children whose emotions can be overwhelming when something is challenging. If your child is showing signs of distress at any point ask yourself what might be causing the distress. Could it be the environment? Is it too loud, hot, cold or windy? Is your child tired? Have you been working on a project for too long? It is possible that your child may be trying to get out of something he doesn't want to do, in which case you can probably push a little more to make it clear that giving up isn't okay in this instance. While this attempt at manipulation may happen occasionally, more often with young kids the crying response has to do with difficulty regulating emotions when something is challenging.

"Children who are pressured, or who have learned to focus only on goals, are less creative, spontaneous, and eager to experiment."

When training bike and ski instructors, I usually tell them that crying is a natural part of a young child's emotional processing and regulation, but panic is not. If your child is crying she may be working through a stress response that is reasonable given the challenge she is facing, but if she is panicked or hysterical (or heading in that direction) then it's past time to take a break and come back to the activity at a later time. If you pay attention, over time you will learn your child's indications when something is too much.

Generally with The Block Plan Preschool you don't need to worry about pushing your child too much as the curriculum is designed to expose your child over time to fun and interesting learning experiences that will add up to a complete preschool education. Try not to worry too much about the outcome of each activity and celebrate when your child tries new things. Ideally we want our children to know their own minds and believe in their power to make choices, but also teach them to be willing to try things outside their existing comfort zones without feeling that they will disappoint us if things don't work out exactly right.

As you are teaching your child the curriculum this year, I hope you will remember that it's all a process and that the outcome that matters most is the learning itself. It doesn't matter what the art projects look like or even which skills and knowledge your child ends the year with. What matters most is that your child has learned to *learn* and knows from his relationship with you that learning is important and fun.

THE BLOCK PLAN PRESCHOOL

COMMON QUESTIONS

Now that we have addressed the philosophies that form the foundation of The Block Plan Preschool, let's answer some questions you may have about how this will work.

WHAT IS THE PURPOSE OF PRESCHOOL?

The purpose of preschool is to prepare children to interact with the world outside your home and immediate family environment, specifically the public (or private) school environment. Preschool is the time of life that children can walk and talk, but are not developmentally ready to attend elementary school. In short, that's the goal of preschool: to get them ready.

While some states and school districts are developing a public preschool system, many are not, and even if there is a public preschool in your neighborhood chances are good it is pretty expensive. So what is a stay-at-home parent in a single-income family to do? You may ask yourself: What does my child really need to learn in preschool? How should I go about preparing him for elementary school? Does he really need to attend an expensive program outside the home? Can I really do this myself?

As a former preschool teacher in many different types of schools I can tell you that most preschools are wonderful whether the curriculum is taught in a day care format or a shorter length program (mornings only, for example). But I can also tell you that the academic curriculum is not rocket science. With some structure and dedication you can prepare your child at home for elementary school, and the purpose of this book is to teach you how to do it. I will give you the tools you need to help your child develop intellectually, physically and emotionally on a timeline that will prepare her for a kindergarten classroom.

Managing a class of 15 students of varying levels of knowledge and ability, designing curriculum and teaching a wide range of skills in a short window of time requires extensive skill, experience and education to be an effective preschool teacher. But that's not what you're doing. You're not teaching preschool, you're teaching your child, and that is very different. You will have only your children as students and you will not have a short period of time to work with them, but instead have all the time in the day. And you do not have to design your own curriculum because you have this book to help you.

This material will provide education on letters, numbers, colors and shapes. We will set up a structure for teaching your child about what they see in the world such as modes of transportation, animals, mountains and the ocean. Your child will learn the art of recitation and presentation to help with the demands of an elementary school classroom. She will learn to recognize her own name, hang up her jacket and open her own snack. Your child will work on character development such as patience, gentleness and kindness. He will practice fine and gross motor skills such as digging, cutting and catching a ball. And within this structure your child will learn to associate abstract concepts, such as an oval shape, with the concrete world he is better able to connect with, such as an egg.

Regardless of what external programs a child attends, he will need to learn at home as well.

WHY SHOULD MY CHILD LEARN AT HOME?

School is a stressful environment for young children. Every child handles it differently, but any day care provider or preschool teacher can tell you that there are significant behavioral differences in children who spend more time in day care and those who spend more time at home. The way your child spends his days is a very personal choice that involves many factors. I am not here to judge your family's choice either way. Instead, I will present the benefits of learning at home either in addition to external programs or in place of them.

In all my years working with children aged two to six years, I can count the number of times on my two hands that a child of five years or older has cried when being dropped off at a school, day care or camp. Whether it is the first day or the hundredth day, a new place or a familiar place, after five years old children rarely cry when dropped off. Between two and four years old, however, it happens all the time. These children cry on predictable days and on unpredictable days. Years of seeing this happen has led to my philosophy that before five years old, management of the stress of the school (or day care or camp) environment is the significant challenge for children leaving less room for learning academic knowledge or skills. This means that for your child to advance academically, she needs to be in a calm, comfortable environment at home.

The value of schools, day cares and camps for children younger than five is largely in learning to be part of a group, exercising emotional regulation, and practicing managing themselves more independently, which are valuable lessons but are not enough to prepare them academically for kindergarten. This means that regardless of what external programs a child attends, he will need to learn at home as well.

In addition to needing a quiet place to advance academic skills, your children need you as parents. They need your presence, your love, your attention, and your example. If you can possibly do it, spend the time to teach your children the skills they will need to interact with the world and you will all benefit. If you put in the effort now, when your kids turn five they will be ready to enter that big world outside your home with confidence and independence. They will have well-developed language and social skills and so will the kids around them, making the social dynamics of schools and camps easier to manage. When your child enters kindergarten she will still need your time, love, attention and support, but if you use The Block Plan Preschool curriculum then she will be well-prepared for the challenges ahead and you will have set a precedent of working on those challenges together.

WHY THE BLOCK PLAN PRESCHOOL?

The Block Plan Preschool is founded on the concept that children do not understand arbitrary concepts that form the foundation of our system of communication, language, and math so they require an immersive experience to help them attach meaning to the letters, numbers and colors they are learning. To a very young child the letter B is a series of squiggly lines. It means nothing more to her than something you are trying to get her to recognize. But when you connect it with meaning such as the Zoo-Phonics character Bubba Bear and focus on the color brown during the month of November when there is brown all around her and you are eating brown food at Thanksgiving like turkey and the peel of potatoes and crunching the brown leaves, suddenly the letter B is something she recognizes.

You have probably heard children described as sponges. Yes, they are sponges in that they are absorbing all the sights, sounds and smells around them constantly. They desperately want to learn and make sense of all of it, but you must use this to your advantage and not expect them to organize it all on their own. You are your child's most influential teacher because you are with him all the time and he will naturally look up to you. You are best able to create experiences and rig his environment so that he associates meaning with the language and math skills he needs to be successful in school and to develop a joyful relationship with learning about his wonderful world.

You are your child's most influential teacher. You are best able to create experiences to help her develop a joyful relationship with learning.

The Block Plan is designed to immerse the student in a world of your design for one month. Everything for that month revolves around themes that recur in all you do and are intertwined in a way that gives meaning to previously arbitrary concepts such as the alphabet or numbers.

At the end of the month or "The Block" you take everything down and reset in order to create a new world with new lessons and themes. For example, your child will learn to associate brown with bears, the letter B and the sound "buh." She will remember a book about Thanksgiving, another with bears in it and the brown squares she painted. This will remind her that squares have four sides and she learned it in

November when it was brown outside and the leaves were crunchy. She'll remember that November starts with N, which makes the "nuh" sound. And so on. Your child's experience in the November curriculum will become part of who she is, so when she goes to kindergarten and the teacher shows her an N, she can recall all the meaning behind the image, running deeper than just memorization. And she will be able to recite the "nuh" sound when shown the letter N, a standard of kindergarten readiness. Each block is an experience your child will not easily forget.

CAN I REALLY TEACH MY CHILD ALL HE NEEDS TO KNOW AT HOME?

Yes, with a framework, discipline and time set aside for instruction you can teach your child what he needs to know at home in lieu of a formal preschool. This book is your greatest resource for doing just that and will cover all the skills you want your child to know in a format that is inspiring to you and creates meaningful experiences for your child. Remember that preschool is, by definition, a time before your child is ready for school. Children of this age are quite ready to learn, but perhaps not ready to go to a school, sit at a desk, practice worksheets, and learn in a group environment. There are many wonderful things about preschool, but it can be tough on kids and can create anxiety for some children that is unnecessary at that age. Kids between the ages of two and five do not need to do homework drills, but they do need to learn to follow directions, wait patiently, recognize letters and numbers, take care of themselves and write their names. They can learn these things at home if you have the time and commitment to teach them.

At $500 to $9,000 per year, formal preschool is far more expensive than this book. The Block Plan Preschool's immersive model is an age-appropriate and effective way for your child to establish kindergarten readiness. Begin this curriculum when you can, as early as 18 months to as late as five years old. Use it to inform your daily routine and the adventures you take with your children. Organize your home and toys around the theme for the month and fill your house with special colors and art projects to create visual and tactile clues throughout your child's environment. Again, you are your child's best teacher and you are best able to rig their early childhood environment for immersive learning.

HOW DO I CHALLENGE MY CHILD APPROPRIATELY?

Every child is precious and unique! Some things will come easily to your child and some will be more challenging, and that's okay. Throughout the curriculum we will discuss what we want your child to know at a minimum and what you can help her pursue if she's showing unusual interest. It's okay to follow your child's interests even if it's temporarily at the expense of something else.

Children develop in a loop-de-loop pattern, they go around in circles while generally progressing forward! This is true physically, cognitively, emotionally and academically.

I am sure you have already witnessed the pattern, for example, when your child is practicing running and all she wants to do is run around everywhere but her language doesn't progress much for a couple weeks. Then once she's mastered the running motor pattern, she'll pick up some new words or develop another skill all of a sudden. That's the loop-de-loop pattern, she works on something at the expense of something else until she's ready to come back to it.

Right now your child might be really interested in shapes and numbers, but that doesn't mean he won't ever think letters and words are interesting. The Block Plan Preschool is designed to be repeated for several years leading up to kindergarten so that eventually you will get to everything. That is the ideal scenario. If you are beginning the curriculum later you will need to be a little more intentional about making sure your child spends adequate time on literacy and math lessons. If you begin early, however, there is nothing to worry about because eventually you will get to it all.

WHAT SHOULD WE WORK TOWARD AT EACH AGE?

As we just discussed, this curriculum is designed to be repeated and added to every year beginning the year your child turns two years old and ending the year your child turns five years old or the last year before your child enters kindergarten. If you feel your child isn't learning enough to be challenged in kindergarten, you can use The Block Plan Preschool curriculum to support that learning as well. Although this schedule is ideal, you don't need to do it this way. I encourage you to use the curriculum in the way it best fits your family so if you have just joined us and your child is five then welcome! This will still work beautifully for your child. And if you are getting started and your child will turn two this year, then welcome! This will work beautifully for your child.

Every year we have different goals for what your child will learn, but while these are recommendations and can help guide you, it's still up to you and your family to decide what you would like to focus on for your particular student.

The Year Your Child Turns Two
Stories and Books
Art Projects and Basic Fine Motor Skills
Calendar
Name Recognition
Recognizing: Colors, Shapes, Letters, Numbers

The Year Your Child Turns Three
All From Previous Year
Zoo-Phonics Animal Sounds and Actions
Counting
Understanding Numbers

Using Scissors and Glue
Introduce Writing Your Name
Exploring Types of Play: Cooperative, Imaginative, Partner, Group, Independent
Songs

The Year Your Child Turns Four

All From Previous Year
Writing Uppercase Letters
Zoo-Phonics Lowercase Letters
Writing Numbers
Months of the Year
Science Projects
Literacy Conversations
Developing Independent Play Skills

The Year Your Child Turns Five

All From Previous Year
Writing Lowercase Letters
Sight Words
Addition and Subtraction
Days of the Week
Worksheet Skills: Tracing, Drawing, Cutting, Crumpling
Developing Group and Cooperative Play Skills

Remember that children will show interest in these skills at different rates and that's okay! Go with what your child wants to do, but be sure to encourage development of skills by adding challenge as your child is able. Keep in mind that it may take repeated exposure to skills or activities before your child will really enjoy them so don't be afraid to try things a couple times even if your child isn't wild about it the first time. It's like trying a new food, the first time it may be new, but the second or third time you might like it! Try your best to be positive, encouraging and supportive as your child learns new skills and gains wonderful knowledge that will stimulate and inspire her to live a life engaged in the world around her! Those are our ultimate goals, more than developing measurable skills on a set timeline.

Try your best to be positive, encouraging and supportive as your child learns new skills and gains wonderful knowledge that will stimulate and inspire her to live a life engaged in the world around her!

Gifted Learners

Gifted learners are a unique group identified and distinguished from other high-achieving children by a specific set of characteristics. Visit the National Association for Gifted Children website www.nagc.org for more information on how to identify a gifted learner.

Do you suspect your child is a gifted learner? If so, you are in the right place as The Block Plan Preschool is particularly well designed for the complexity of thought, visual-spacial learning style, sensitivity, and intrinsic motivation typical of the gifted child. If you notice your child wanting to learn ever more even as a toddler and exhibiting signs of complexity of thought it is a great time to begin The Block Plan Preschool curriculum lessons no matter the age of your child.

The visual-spacial learning style means that gifted children often work from whole to part instead of step-by-step. This means they need to understand and view the big picture from the outset and then will explore lessons in smaller parts. Most educational systems do not accommodate this and instead work in a step-by-step method ("Gifted Education: School Issues"). By working within the framework of our monthly themes, focus pages, book lists, and experiential field trips and activities, all lessons have a broader meaning as part of the larger block.

The quiet, calm environment of your home will allow your child to learn without having to manage a loud and distracting classroom environment, which is particularly difficult for gifted children who experience sensitivity to light, sound and behaviors of other children.

The intrinsic motivation typical of gifted learners is perfectly suited to The Block Plan Preschool's flexible choice learning plan where children can explore subject matter at their own pace and in whatever depth they choose. Parents are given all the tools necessary to accommodate and maximize learning opportunities for gifted children, all they need to do is begin at a young age and keep adding challenges as their children grow up during the early childhood years.

The Block Plan Preschool can be adapted for all preschool-age children and is an exceptionally useful resource for families of gifted children.

KINDERGARTEN READINESS

"School readiness involves more than just children. School readiness, in the broadest sense, is about children, families, early environments, schools, and communities. Children are not innately ready or not ready for school. Their skills and development are strongly influenced by their families and through their interactions with other people and environments before coming to school."

– Kelly L. Maxwell, Ph.D. and Richard M. Clifford, Ph.D,
Authors of "School Readiness Assessment,"
an Article Referenced by the NAEYC
in a Position Paper on School Readiness

Kindergarten or school readiness has to do with more than what knowledge your child possesses, although this is certainly part of it. School readiness refers to cognition, social skills, self-care skills, emotional regulation and awareness, ability to recite knowledge and answer questions, fine and large motor skills, neurological health, and ability to trust others and engage in healthy social relationships. Your child needs a wide range of fun, healthy, positive, engaging experiences with you and other people in order to be fully ready for school. If you choose to use them, formal preschools and preparatory programs are only one part of the kindergarten readiness equation, while the rest of it happens at home.

LITERACY AND MATH

"In our own studies, and in those of others, we have found that what is crucial to beginning to read is the child's attachment to an adult who spends time reading to or with the child. The motivation for reading, which is a difficult task, is social."

— David Elkind, *The Hurried Child*

LITERACY

One of the first things your child will probably do in kindergarten is to begin skills testing with most of it focused on literacy. At most schools, in the first couple weeks of school your child will be taken aside by a paraeducator or teacher and will be tested on basic literacy skills. These test results will likely determine which reading group or level your child will be placed in for the entirety of the kindergarten year. Because we want your child to be challenged in kindergarten, you should spend time during preschool years working toward the basic elements of literacy and add more advanced elements as your child requires more challenge. It is not enough for your child to know the information, she must be able to recount it out loud on demand to an adult she may not know very well.

The knowledge and skills your child needs to meet these literacy goals are found in the curriculum. You do not need to create extra lessons or projects, but simply follow the program and keep these goals in mind throughout your child's preschool years.

Basic elements of literacy at the kindergarten level are: recognizing upper-case and lower-case letters by sight, looking at upper-case and lower-case letters and making the corresponding sounds, and recognizing and writing the child's own first and last name. Ideally your child will have these skills mastered before entering kindergarten and will feel comfortable performing these tasks in front of a teacher one-on-one.

More advanced elements of literacy at this age are writing upper-case and lower-case letters, making sounds of combinations of letters (sh, th, ch, etc.), recognizing sight words, reading actual words and phrases, writing words and phrases, and working with language patterns such as rhyming and opposites (the weather is not hot, it is _____). The advanced elements of literacy are longer-term objectives that your child will work toward during her kindergarten year. They are good to keep in mind and useful to add to your child's curriculum for additional challenge, but are not meant to cause you stress thinking this is what your child needs to know before beginning school.

The Block Plan Preschool curriculum will incorporate these elements of literacy and help you develop a solid foundation for reading and writing with your child. We will use fine motor skill development to support hand strength used for holding a pencil; practice recognizing words by sight at a very young age beginning with your family's names; use Zoo-Phonics to add meaning to the sounds and shapes letters make; and use Handwriting Without Tears to practice drawing letters. With practice your child will master these basic literacy skills and more, and he will be well-prepared for that first round of testing in kindergarten with comfort and confidence in his knowledge and abilities.

It is not enough for your child to know the information, she must be able to recount it out loud on demand to an adult she may not know very well.

See below for an excerpt of the Pre-K Skills Assessment in *The Block Plan Preschool: Preparing Your Child at Home for Kindergarten*. The assessment is designed to prepare your child for the testing he will encounter in kindergarten.

Relationships

Can you put the cube inside the cup? _____

Can you put the cube on the cup? _____

Can you put the cube next to the cup? _____

Can you put the cube below the cup? _____

Can you put the cube above the cup? _____

Mark if your child completes the action correctly and any relevant notes. Some of these may look the same depending on your child's interpretation, such as on the cup and above the cup, which is fine. If you want to add challenge to this activity you can give compound directions (with multiple parts) to give your child practice following multiple directions in correct succession. That would sound like this, "Can you put the cup on the table and then put the cube on the cup?"

*What is opposite of...

hot? _____	low? _____
short? _____	day? _____
slow? _____	big? _____
dark? _____	

There aren't necessarily perfectly correct answers to these, so mark your child's answer as correct if they get the general idea and feel free to make up your own examples. This is essentially an advanced skill and not every child will master this before kindergarten, and that's okay.

MATH

Similar to the process for assigning literacy groups, your child will likely undergo initial testing in the first couple of weeks of school and be placed into a math group. This is highly important as math groups can sometimes be split into different classrooms and may learn completely different information for the duration of the year.

Math testing will cover the following basic skills: counting to 10 (memorization and counting actual objects), recognizing numbers 1-10 by sight, identifying names of shapes, and replicating patterns (red, yellow, blue, red, yellow, _____). More advanced math skills include very basic addition and subtraction (usually using tangible objects and recounting them), counting to 100, writing numbers 1-20, and creating new patterns.

In order to prepare your child for math testing you will want to practice recitation of her skills as she will need to perform on demand with a paraeducator or teacher in the same way she did with the literacy testing. The Block Plan Preschool curriculum will teach your child basic math skills and will offer extra lessons you can use to challenge your child with advanced math skills as needed. Remember that math symbols and concepts are representative and can be challenging for some kids to master. It is okay if your child has trouble with it, but try to add meaning if he seems to be having trouble remembering or understanding the concepts. Practice identifying patterns in nature or in your home before practicing them with blocks or on paper and make sure you are counting objects instead of just reciting 1-10, which can end up being a kind of counting "song."

The Block Plan Preschool will help you identify shapes in your daily life with your child and will provide you opportunities to count toys, wheels, eyes, toes, sides on each shape and many other things to help assign numbers some meaning. By promoting understanding of math concepts in this way, practicing these skills and adding in recitation practice during the final preschool year, your child will be ready for that initial math test in kindergarten.

The curriculum will provide you opportunities to count toys, wheels, eyes, toes, sides on shapes and many other things to help assign numbers some meaning.

SELF-CARE

When your child begins kindergarten she will be expected to maintain a level of independent self-care throughout the day. Of course, adults will be there to assist her, but for the most part that will be an exception rather than a rule. You cannot expect, for example, that an adult will be available to wipe your child's bottom in the bathroom or open his snack every day. Unless it is a significant problem, your child's teacher may never bring these issues up with you, but it will create problems for your child if he is not prepared to take care of himself during the day. The teacher or paraeducator will help your child open his snack or lunch, for example, but it will take some time and will affect your child's sense of independence and confidence. It may even be embarrassing for him in front of classmates. So, do your child a favor and follow the guidelines below for various areas of self-care so that she can be confident in kindergarten!

> **Beginning around 18 months old your child can do a maneuver called, "The Flip," in order to put her own jacket on.**

SIMPLICITY

Our general rule for self-care is to make it as simple for your child as possible. We don't want a lot of moving parts, things need to fit in the backpack and lunchbox. We don't want unnecessary extras going to school with your child like loveys, toys, extra shoes or extra jackets. You don't want to give your child more things than she can handle and give her lots of things she can lose. If you want it to come home, label it! And make sure your child knows what's important. For example, it might be okay if you lose your water bottle, but not your snow boots! You need to prioritize with children, they can keep track of some things, but not everything. It is not an appropriate expectation for you to think that they will not lose things. They will and it has to do with their age and stage of brain development and there is nothing you can do about it. Except to keep it simple for them! Keeping it simple will minimize loss (a nice benefit for you) and increase confidence and self-sufficiency, both important aspects of kindergarten readiness.

LAYERS OF CLOTHING

Teach your child at a young age to put on his jacket and take it off. Zippers are easier than snaps or buttons, so that cute jacket with wooden toggles may look great to you, but do him a favor and get him a jacket he can zip himself. Beginning around 18 months old your child can do a maneuver called, "The Flip," in order to put her jacket on. Lay the jacket open and face-up on the floor in front of your child, hood near the feet. Show your child to put her hands in the sleeves of her jacket, then flip the jacket up over her head and her arms will slide into the sleeves. Even if she can't zip it on her own, getting her coat on and off is something she should be able to do by the age of two. You will likely need to put your own coat on this way in order to set an example and assist learning until your child masters The Flip. The steps are: hood by my feet, arms in sleeves and do the flip!

Your child must also be able to hang up his jacket on a hook neatly. This is something you can easily practice in your own home and should be part of your arrival routine in your home preschool. Hang a hook somewhere in your home at a low level so your child can practice managing her coat every time you leave and reenter your home. This will probably take some extra time, especially at first, but will be an important investment in the future of self-care for your child and eventually you will be so happy when you can say, "We're leaving in five minutes, please go put on your jacket!" And your two-year-old will likely be able to do it!

You should also make sure your child is dressed in layers that he can manage on his own. While your child is crawling I prefer sweatshirts and clothes that are smooth, without zippers, buttons, snaps or hoods that do not impede movement or irritate her skin. Crawling is actually an important activity for healthy brain development as it helps the connection between both sides of the brain develop into a super high-way with fast, efficient communication, so crawling should be a fun, playful activi-ty for your child to continue even when she is walking! Clothing should encourage movement and never discourage it. Once your child is capable of managing her own body temperature, usually around two and a half or three years old, you can move to zippered layers so that she can get them on with The Flip and take them off when desired. By kindergarten your child should be dressing herself easily, but it is still up to you to make sure she has breathable, functional, comfortable layers to wear through-out the day. The temperature will swing quite a bit in schools from warm to cold, so make sure your child knows how to monitor his body temperature and put things on and take them off in order to manage it.

Your child will need shoes that are appropriate for gym class and outdoor recess.

SHOES
Similar to managing a jacket, your child will need to manage her shoes on her own. Until your child can tie her own shoelaces, do her a favor and buy only shoes she can put on by herself meaning Velcro or slip on! I know there are so many adorable options that seem like they should be fine, but ties and zippers before your child has mastered them for himself are only making both your lives more complicated and frustrating. Your child will also need shoes that are appropriate for gym class and outdoor recess. While it is okay to send separate gym shoes or separate snow boots, I recommend finding some multi-purpose shoes so that your child will not have to change during the day.

It can be stressful for a five-year-old to come in from recess and try to manage changing shoes in addition to getting a drink of water, taking off his jacket and other layers and getting to his desk while the teacher is beginning instruction. Your child's teacher will not be able to help with this and will likely get frustrated with your child if he has too much to handle and cannot do it efficiently. Same goes for changing shoes for gym class. There is no time set aside for this in class, so your child will likely have to stay behind with a paraeducator or other classroom helper (if one is available) while the class goes on to gym. This is stressful for students and teachers and can cause frustration in even the most patient of people. So do your child a favor and send him to school in good footwear that fits the conditions and needs of the day. Your child needs to be free to run and play at any moment during the school day! It is not a fashion show and if you set the rule, I'm sure your child will get used to the idea of "school shoes."

My favorite brands of shoes are Riley Roos (for toddlers), BOGS (versatile waterproof boots for all ages), Crocs or Natives (mostly for warmer weather, but can be great before kids can manipulate fasteners), TOMS (also for warmer weather and no fasteners), and Nike Frees (with foam soles, let those feet move naturally!). By the time your child gets to kindergarten a pair of BOGS for wet and snowy days and a pair of athletic shoes such as Nike Frees should do the job. They make both BOGS and Nike Frees in fun colors to satisfy even picky kids and both are versatile, useful for the playground and will work great for gym class. The great thing about BOGS is that they are warm and waterproof, but can be pulled on easily and have a low-profile sole so that your child can still run in them. The best prices for these shoes are usually on Zulily or at a discount store such as Nordstrom Rack or DSW. I keep an eye on these places and buy shoes in sizes ahead of my child so when he grows out of a size I have a new one all ready to go that I bought at a sale price so that we are not usually caught needing something when there are no sales going on.

Obviously, you should teach your child zippers, shoelaces, snaps and buttons as soon as he is capable of learning. This is your responsibility. My husband's family never taught him to tie shoelaces so he figured it out for himself and still ties his shoes in a unique way I've never seen before. This is not something to let your child figure out on his own, but something for you to practice together.

Everything your child takes to school should fit inside a small backpack that she can easily pack and carry herself.

BACKPACK
Everything your child takes to school should fit inside a small backpack that she can easily pack and carry herself. Your child will likely have a school folder to bring back

The Pygmalion Effect

Every teacher, no matter how fair-minded and loving will have favorite students. It comes down to our humanness and the fact that people always connect with some people more than others. It is only the teacher's fault if she consciously changes her behavior toward some students based on her feelings about them, but this is not usually the case. Teacher's expectations and preferences for students usually operates on a subconscious level, which is difficult to do anything about.

In a 1960s experiment Robert Rosenthal and Lenore Jacobson found that the effects of teacher expectations are profound on student performance, especially in younger children. Rosenthal's study randomly identified certain students as gifted and gave the results to teachers. Although the students were randomly chosen, teachers thought the results were real. Amazingly, by the end of the school year the "gifted" students were performing to the expectations of their teachers at a level higher than their peers. This self-fulfilling prophecy is called the Pygmalion effect. Through additional research Rosenthal found that teachers subconsciously treated students differently when they expected them to succeed (Rosenthal and Jacobson, 1966).

I have seen this happen first hand in my own classroom. A few months into teaching my first preschool class a colleague asked me who my favorite student was. I hadn't thought much about it up to that point, but when asked I identified one student for whom I had a preference. To my knowledge, I did not change my behavior toward that student or any other, but I began to see a remarkable change in the weeks following that conversation. This student positively blossomed. She began to come alive in class becoming more engaged and affectionate whereas she had been more quiet and reserved before. By the end of our school year, this student was bounding joyfully into class and when she had to move on to a new class with a different teacher she reverted back to being quiet, reserved and in fact made that teacher's life very difficult.

Due to Rosenthal's research, I know that this student coming alive in school had to do with my preference for her and high expectations of her performance. Your child will not be a teacher's favorite every year he is in school, but setting him up for success before school even starts will help that relationship get off on the right foot. And as we have learned, the relationship between your child and his first teachers can have an extraordinary effect on him and his performance in school.

and forth, a snack, a lunch, maybe gloves and a hat, and a water bottle. She will probably have a cubby or hook on which to hang her things, which should be a jacket and backpack at most. Too many loose items, including extra shoes and a lunchbox that does not fit inside a backpack, is asking for trouble and for things to be lost.

You will want to label important and expensive things and make sure they easily fit inside your child's backpack. Mabel's Labels makes some great labels for all your child's items as teachers and caregivers should not be relied upon to remember what belongs to whom, and your child will probably not be able to keep track of this until first or second grade. I especially like the Preschool Shoe Labels by Mabel's Labels, which help identify the left shoe from right. You can also do this by ordering an oval sticker with your child's name from a company such as Vistaprint and cutting it in half so that the first name is in one shoe and the last name is in the other. Make sure to choose an animal shape, such as a whale, so that your child knows how to fit the pieces together. You do not need to label school supplies from the teacher's list in kindergarten because they are usually combined into a classroom collection since children do not have separate desks at this age.

It does not behoove you to shorten your child's available time for eating.

FOOD

Your precious little one will need to be able to eat snack in about five minutes and lunch in about 15-20 minutes while at school. This includes opening packages, eating, throwing away or recycling waste, and cleaning up his area. For everyone's sake, please pack your child's snack in a container he can open himself. This may mean taking food out of packaging and putting it into a different container, but it will be worth it in the long run for your child's confidence, self-sufficiency and relationship to teachers. While there will likely be someone available to help your child, they are usually also meant to help up to a hundred other children at the same time so it does not behoove you to shorten your child's available time for eating. Nor will it do anyone any good to try the patience of your child's teachers, paraeducators and teaching assistants.

When working as a paraeducator for kindergarten I once had a child who brought lunches made up entirely of packaged items everyday. The problem wasn't that the food wasn't healthy; his lunches included items such as crackers, string cheese and pre-cut apple slices. The problem was that he couldn't open a single item himself so he had to wait at least five minutes for me to come help him open five to six packages each day before he could even start eating his lunch. This means he had less than 10 minutes to eat every day and no way to put everything back in his lunch box without making a big mess. While I understand this strategy was probably an easy way for his parents to pack a healthy lunch, it really wasn't great for the child in the long run.

So, what works? I love PlanetBox lunch and snack boxes for children! Children ages three and up can open them easily, they are great sizes, slide easily into backpacks, and they are made of one piece that is super easy to clean each day. PlanetBox and any other quality snack or lunch system is an investment, but your child can use it for the rest of her life. As an adult, I took my lunch in a PlanetBox for years and it still functions perfectly and looks as good as new. In addition to ease of use and self-sufficiency for children, another advantage to using a system such as PlanetBox is that it clearly lays out what you have packed for lunch and is likely to inspire you to pack fresh, lovely food. In the Rover model (perfect size for kids and the one I use even as an adult) is a compartment for a sandwich, a fruit, a vegetable, a small treat and a snack and it is all laid out before you. Beautiful. You could buy some of PlanetBox's smaller containers for a snack until your child needs to pack a full lunch for school and still practice the easy system. The carry bags also sold by PlanetBox work great by providing a spot for a drink and handle for carrying as your child will need to carry his lunch down the hall, to the lunch room, out to the playground and then back into the classroom. If you give your child too much to keep track of on this journey, they are nearly guaranteed to lose something at some point.

Remember our general rule about self-care: make it as simple as possible. We want the fewest moving parts when it comes to food. Children feel terrible when they lose things you want them to keep track of, and truly it is not developmentally appropriate for us to expect them to come home with everything they are sent out with every single time. Kids lose things and while we want them to learn from it, it is a waste to make them feel badly because there is nothing they can do about it. They are simply too young to keep control of all their belongings all the time. But we can make it as easy for them as possible by labeling the things that are important to us and giving them well-designed, developmentally appropriate things to work with.

Remember our general rule about self-care: make it as simple as possible.

Sending your child to school with a bunch of separate containers with separate lids and, worse, all different sizes is a recipe for frustration for you, for the child and for the teacher. A child of this age will spend at least two or three minutes just opening all the containers, longer if he needs to ask for help from a teacher. Then it will take at least five minutes to close up the containers, which he will not likely be able to do or plan for, leaving him only five to eight minutes to eat lunch. So he'll be late and will end up throwing everything into his lunchbox (sticky icky mess), leaving containers or lids on the table or even throwing away the container itself. Try a simple lunchbox like the PlanetBox and you will thank yourself everyday. Your child's teacher and your child would thank you too if they knew to do it! The sad truth is that if things are running well no one will think of what you have done to make it go smoothly, but we will know! Your community of Block Plan parents recognize your effort!

BATHROOM

Ahh the bathroom, the favorite place of every parent of a young child. Obviously your goal is to get your child completely potty trained and self-sufficient in all bathroom matters before kindergarten. While most children can accomplish this in some form or another, most will have some kind of incident or challenge at some point during the kindergarten year. While this is okay and age-appropriate, you will want to teach your child how to handle it before sending her off to school. Most teachers will not have the time or resources to personally help a child who has a messy toilet accident, so your child will likely be sent to the nurse's office if things aren't going smoothly. This can be a full-on pee your pants kind of incident or a didn't wipe well and got poop on yourself kind of incident. If there is an actual mess in the bathroom then the janitorial staff will come in to clean it up.

Most children will have some kind of bathroom incident or challenge at some point during the kindergarten year.

All of these things can be embarrassing for young kids so do your best to prepare them for what can happen. Help your child learn to wipe herself by four years old. No one in any child care situation (camps, ski school, etc.) is going to want to help a four year old wipe for child abuse prevention reasons. For children under the age of four the state licensure is different and caregivers are usually familiar with potty training and diapers and are specifically trained in early childhood care. Over the age of four, however, your kid is pretty much on his own in the bathroom when away from you. So let your child practice at home, in a safe environment and let her do it herself even if it makes a mess. It is far better for your little one to make her messes at home than to make them in front of her classmates at school, even if it's tempting for you to help out when it's messy.

Even with all the practice in the world, your child will probably pee his pants or get poop on himself at some point in school. Teach him to approach his teacher right away after an incident, or if he's still in the bathroom, to call to another student to get the teacher for help. Make sure he knows that it might happen, it's nothing to be embarrassed about and it will all be fine. What you don't want is for your child to try to clean up a messy poop and get it all over the walls. Poop on the wall is the worst scenario and will get the most attention. Teach your child not to walk out of the bathroom with his pants down. It is far better to yell for help from inside the bathroom and get the attention of one child than it is to walk into a class with no pants. If your child's classroom does not have its own bathroom then teach your child to pull up her pants no matter the mess inside and walk to the nurse's office. You don't want your child sitting in the bathroom paralyzed with fear until the teacher sends someone to go check on her. Tell her to just pull up her pants and go to the office. If it's a mess then the nurse will help her get cleaned up and changed into clean clothes.

Ask your school what they do in case of a potty accident, some will keep a change of clothes in the nurses office, some will call you to bring something over and some will ask you to pack a change of clothes in your child's backpack. Generally it's a good idea to pack a pair of underwear and pants inside a plastic zip bag in your child's backpack anyway. Choose a pair of slim pants like leggings or thin sweats to be appropriate for a wide range of temperatures and stuff it in the bottom of the bag so it doesn't get pulled out by accident.

Sometimes your child will do something embarrassing like sit in a puddle on the playground and he will want to change into this spare pair of pants. Let your child know what your guidelines are about changing clothes. Usually I leave kids in wet-with-water clothes unless they are sopping wet and it's cold outside or if it's embarrassing like a wet spot that looks like they peed. It is important that your child gets used to some discomfort because she will have some of that while at school all day. You can help her practice this at home by teaching her not to change her shirt when it has a damp sleeve or by waiting for damp socks to dry without changing them. As with all kindergarten readiness lessons, explain to your child why you are making him do this as he will learn to respect the fact that you are preparing him for school and not just being mean.

Do your best to keep self-care simple for your child, prepare him for how to manage mistakes and things that will happen in school and you will have a confident, self-sufficient, kindergarten-ready child on your hands!

CONFLICT RESOLUTION

An important part of kindergarten readiness is the ability to resolve conflict without adult intervention. Children will have access to support from adults, of course, in elementary school, but for the most part they will need to resolve minor disputes on their own with grace, humility and self-respect.

First, you will need to practice a rhetoric or dialogue with your child to give him the tools to resolve conflicts with peers and express his feelings. I worked with a kindergarten teacher once who taught his students to "check in" with each other when they are feeling upset. So Olivia would approach Daniel and say, "Daniel, I need a check in." Daniel is not allowed to say no to this, one must always grant a check in. Daniel would say, "Okay I am ready to listen," so that Olivia knows she has his attention. Then Olivia would tell Daniel what she is feeling. For example, "My feelings are hurt from when you pushed me out of the way to get to the slide." Then comes the important part. No matter Daniel's age he must use three components of an apology to resolve this conflict and repair the relationship with his peer. The components are: intention, remorse and amends.

To address intention Daniel must let Olivia know that he did not hurt her on purpose. This is especially important with young children because there is nothing more hurtful to them than someone hurting them on purpose. As we grow older we realize that sometimes this happens and we have more tools in our emotional toolbox to handle it, but a young child needs to know that nobody tried to harm them on purpose. They are so fresh out of the ego development phase (realizing that there are other people apart and separate from them but also the same as far as feelings and self-importance) that the concept that someone would purposely put them in harm's way is nearly inconceivable. There is a little part of your young child that still thinks she is the sun and everything orbits around her and this is okay. It's a normal arc of development for children to realize that this is not the case (Santrock, 2007). But at the ages of two, three, four, five and even six years old it is of paramount importance that the offender, and in many cases both children, verbally state that they did not mean to hurt the offended.

> **No matter Daniel's age, he must use three components of an apology to resolve this conflict and repair the relationship with his peer. The components are: intention, remorse and amends.**

Next (or more often first), Daniel must express remorse. We all know what it's like to receive an apology that does not seem genuine. Young children don't quite have the radar for that yet so all they need to hear is, "I'm sorry." That is a huge roadblock for young children. You must say you're sorry right away or you're not getting anywhere, they will not even hear anything you have to say if you don't first express remorse. This is usually the first thing babies learn to do. As early as 18 months you can teach your child to give gentle touch by stroking another person's arm and saying, "I'm sorry." This is the foundation and beginning of his conflict resolution skill development.

It is very important to us as parents to teach our children how to make it right.

Now Daniel must make amends. This is something that not all educators will teach your child or impress upon other children as the first two components are often enough to put a Band-Aid on the situation. It is very important to us as parents, however, to teach our children to make it right. If you make a mistake or offend someone, even by accident, you must make it up to that person in order to build or preserve a close relationship with them. I'm sure we've all had the experience of forgiving someone, but growing apart from them after a conflict that never got to this stage. You must learn at an early age to repair your mistakes. It's okay to make them, but you have to put in the effort to make it better. This is also true at home, it's okay if your child spills milk, but teach her to clean it up starting at about 18 months. You don't need to make her clean all of it up at that age, but tell her that it's okay to spill then give her a rag and encourage her to help you wipe it up.

So what does this look like all put together? Not as complicated as you might think. I teach this in my classrooms, "I'm sorry, I didn't mean to hurt you, what can I do to help you feel better?" By the end of the school year those phrases echo all around my classroom during free play and I no longer need to be part of the resolution. The kids are doing it themselves and building strong friendships, it's truly amazing to watch your child do this on their own the first time. And the second. And the third! So the entire conversation in a preschool classroom might go something like this:

Olivia: Miss Katy! (crying) Daniel pushed me!
Miss Katy: Did you talk to him about it?
O: No. (stops crying)
Miss Katy: I'm sorry that happened sweetheart, but you need to talk to *him* about it, not me.
Olivia runs over to Daniel and tries to get his attention.
Daniel keeps playing.
O: Daniel, I need a check in.
Daniel stops and turns to her.
D: Okay, I am ready to listen.
O: My feelings are hurt from when you pushed me out of the way to get to the slide.
D: I'm sorry, I didn't mean to hurt you, what can I do to help you feel better?
O: Let me have a turn on the slide.
D: Okay! Guys, it's Olivia's turn!

They both run to the slide together happily and Olivia takes a turn down the slide. All is forgiven.

This can be quite surprising the first time you see it happen because the solutions children come up with are not what we would think of or suggest. The example above probably makes sense to you, Olivia misses her turn on the slide and has hurt feelings so Daniel apologizes and gives her a turn on the slide and she is fine. Many times, however, especially with younger kids the solutions will seem bizarre to you. Kids may say that a hug makes them feel better or getting them a paper towel will help or they want to play with trucks together. This may not make sense to you, but it makes sense to them 99% of the time. The other child will say, "Okay!" No matter how unrelated the request and they will have a renewed love for each other. These exchanges can be so funny and yet are so important. Children are practicing the art of resolving conflict and you must let them do it in their own childish style, both with you and with other young children.

Practice this dialogue with your child as if you are reading from a script. Young children need the tools and don't know what to say so you must teach them exactly what to say. That's the purpose of the highly repeatable phrase, "I'm sorry, I didn't mean to hurt you, what can I do to help you feel better?" Practice that with your child until he can recite it like a robot. It sounds funny, but that's how we learn social rhetoric, by practicing and repeating what we hear others say. So next time you have a conflict with your child say the phrase to her and do what she asks you to do to fix it. You may need to give her some ideas about what will help her feel better the first few times. Then when your child does something that makes you feel upset or hurt say these words, "Honey, say to me, 'Mommy, I'm sorry, I didn't mean to hurt you, what can I do to help you feel better?'" And then after he apologizes, tell him, "Thank you for apologizing, I will feel better if you _____."

Practice this dialogue with your child as if you are reading from a script. Young children need the tools and don't know what to say so you must teach them exactly what to say.

As a parent it is important to thank your child for apologizing. Try not to excuse the behavior by saying, "It's okay." If you're going through a conflict resolution process, then whatever the behavior was, it's not okay! But you will get past it and the first step is a true apology by addressing our three components: intention, remorse and amends. Kids don't usually need to make this distinction with each other, but we need to make it with our kids and with other adults. You ran into my car because you were texting and driving, I won't tell you it's okay, it's not okay! But I will thank you for apologizing every single time. Same with your kids.

So, as stay-at-home parents how do we provide opportunity to practice this with other children? What if you only have one child? Use your play groups and time in public places like playgrounds to let your child work this out. You can speak to the adults about it and tell them that you are trying to give your child an opportunity to work out conflict on her own so you will not intervene at first if something comes up, but it doesn't mean you're not paying attention. Even if they are strangers you can tell them the language you have taught your child to use, maybe they will teach their child too. Try to spend time with other parents who agree with your philosophy and allow your children to hit, bump or insult each other by accident and then work out the ensuing conflict by themselves. I know that sounds terrible, but accidents happen and your child needs to learn to deal with them. It will be okay! Again, you can do this as early as 18 months and I suggest you do. It may be that you have a hard time finding other parents who are on board with this, but keep trying because it will benefit your child.

Imagine that you are a teacher in a classroom with 15 kids playing all around you. It would be impossible to intervene in every interaction that goes on during indoor play or on the playground and it's okay that you don't as long as you are supporting and teaching them when they need help. As we have learned, children need this time to practice managing their emotions and navigating tricky interpersonal relationships. And they will learn to do it, but you need to give them the tools and then let them try on their own. They won't do it perfectly every time, but perfection is usually not necessary and they will be able to work it out in their own special way.

When you are with other parents allow your children to play together in another room or a place that you know is safe that is a little bit removed from you. Then let the kids come to you when they need help, giving them a chance to work through conflict on their own.

Find a group of friends that is committed to this, practice the dialogue with your child (yes, you need to do it like you are reading from a script!) and you will help your child be ready for the social aspects of kindergarten.

MAKING IT WORK FOR YOUR FAMILY

"Whatever you can do or dream you can, begin it. Boldness has genius, power and magic in it. Begin it now."

– Johann Wolfgang von Goethe

My dad always says, "There's never a wrong time to do the right thing." You may not feel that you have everything in order right now and that's okay, begin it anyway! It doesn't matter if you have all the books, if it's the middle of the school year, or if you feel your child isn't the exact right age, begin it anyway! Don't feel that everything must be perfect for The Block Plan Preschool to work for your family; use what works for you today, change it if you need to, and leave the rest. The following chapters will help you make decisions that are right for you, your family and your child. Now, let's begin!

GETTING STARTED

This curriculum draws on existing educational tools that your child will use in the public school classroom. Some materials and supplies you will need to gather yourself such as Zoo-phonics flash cards and a Handwriting Without Tears workbook. Nearly every homeschool curriculum package you look into is more expensive than this book and includes proprietary books, craft materials and worksheets. I know you are smart and you can cut out the letter Z from construction paper.

There are plenty of wonderful classic and contemporary books out there that make up a rich body of children's literature to use in your lessons so I've included book lists for each month. Going to the library with your child and choosing books for the month's curriculum is a wonderful learning experience and if you don't have access to a good library, all of these books are available for purchase online, either new or used. Gathering your collection of materials will take some time, but you don't need to it all at once. One of the benefits of beginning The Block Plan Preschool early and repeating it year after year is that you will begin simply with your young child and add to your lessons (and materials) as your child grows older. I have put together a list to make it as easy as possible for you to get started on this great learning adventure. Trust me, it's much less expensive and better for your family than if I sent you a preassembled kit!

WHAT DO I NEED?
See the following section (page 43) for a convenient checklist of all the materials and supplies you will need for a year of curriculum. Below is an explanation of each material if you need more information or a recommendation for a specific product. The product numbers, availability and prices described are estimates only and are subject to change.

Begin simply with your young child and add to your lessons (and materials) as your child grows older.

LEARNING RESOURCES:
THIS BOOK
Use this book to make your decisions and design your curriculum for each month. I've written a monthly model for you with descriptions of alternate activities. Make your plans and stick to them as best you can, even if you have to rearrange your days a little bit to make sure you hit on every activity and plan you made ahead of time. For best results, finish your monthly lesson plans by the 15th of the preceding month so you have time to get everything set up and/or purchased ahead of time. Pretend you are turning it in for review or actually give a copy of your plan to your spouse and talk it over for a few quick minutes. This may help your partner feel more involved

in your child's education and can actually be helpful in scheduling as some activities take place outside the home. Make sure you work together with your spouse so that you feel supported as the primary educator and to ensure everyone at home is on board with the immersive education experience. For example, you want your spouse to know that in February you are learning about sliding with a focus on either sledding or skiing so that they can take your kids sledding on a weekend morning knowing that it's part of their education.

You don't need to have every single book on the list.

CHILDREN'S BOOKS
The curriculum includes an extensive list of children's literature. For each month there is a book list provided after the month's title page. Although it would be ideal, you don't need to have every single book on the list. Begin by collecting the books for literacy lessons (marked as such on the Book List) and then gather the books for the main curriculum. You don't need the books for Extra Lessons unless you plan to do them (also marked on the Book List). You can purchase the books if you like or check them out from your local library. I usually do a mix of both; I purchase a new book or two per month each year, send the book list to family and friends to use in purchasing gifts for holidays and birthdays, and check the rest out from the library.

A CALENDAR
You will want a calendar with removable numbers so your child can make changes as the days pass. Find a calendar set with days of the week, months, holidays, even weather dials to help take inventory of what is happening that day and week with your child at circle time. DK Classroom Outlet has many affordable calendar sets available on their website (www.dkclassroomoutlet.com) and Melissa and Doug makes a few magnetic versions. Many preschool classrooms choose a theme for the entire school year such as monsters, apples or dinosaurs, but you don't necessarily need to do this because we will be changing themes each month. For more detailed purchasing information and product recommendations visit The Block Plan Preschool blog at www.blockplanpreschool.com/theblog.

ZOO-PHONICS
Zoo-phonics is a wonderful literacy program used in many preschools and public kindergarten programs. It's designed to teach children to associate letters with animal characters that help them learn sounds and draw the letter shapes. By using the Zoo-phonics program at home as part of our curriculum you will create a bridge for your child between your at-home Block Plan Preschool program and the public program he will enter in elementary school. Using these same characters throughout early literacy learning will be beneficial to your child, to you and to your child's future teachers. Our program uses the Small Animal Alphabet Cards and optional Zoo-Coloring Book "a-z" found on the Zoo-Phonics website (www.zoo-phonics.com).

HANDWRITING WITHOUT TEARS: LETTERS AND NUMBERS FOR ME

This handbook is available on the Handwriting Without Tears website at www.hwtears.com. You will need it for the 3-, 4- and 5-year-old instruction years. If you plan to use it for multiple years I would suggest making copies or scanning the pages so that you can reuse the workbook pages for practice.

You will create a bridge for your child between your at-home Block Plan Preschool program and the public program he will enter in elementary school.

MUSIC

I include music exercises and games using two CDs by Greg & Steve, "Kids in Action" and "Kids in Motion." At this time they are not available for purchase in an MP3 form, so you must order the physical disc from www.gregandsteve.com or Amazon. Yes they are older and can seem a little dorky, but they are fun and kids love them!

CREATE YOUR SPACE

Simulating a school environment in your home will help your child feel comfortable and confident in her kindergarten classroom when she gets there. Don't be shy about getting your child ready for "school" by walking around the block and reentering your house as a classroom. You could also have your child get ready for school in her bedroom and then come join you in the part of your house you have designated as your classroom. You may feel silly doing this at home, but remember that kids love to pretend! And they need to practice.

A HOOK OR CUBBY

Your child needs to be able to manage his things, especially a backpack, jacket, water bottle and snack or lunch. In kindergarten your child will likely sit at a table (her place marked with her name) in a chair and have a cubby with a hook (also marked with her name). It isn't until later that most schools provide a desk with storage for students and even then they are likely to hang up jackets and backpacks. It is a good idea to create an environment for your child to practice arriving at school wearing a backpack and jacket, taking them off, hanging them up and taking his place in the "classroom." IKEA has many storage pieces available you can use for this by adding a stick-on or screw-in hook.

A CARPET OR RUG

In a traditional preschool your child would have "circle time" that takes place on a designated rug or carpet in the classroom. Often children have a special assigned spot or everyone sits around the outside of the rug so that they can all see the teacher when he or she reads books or does instruction on the cork board. For just one or two children you do not need an expensive preschool carpet, but it would be nice for your child to practice taking her spot for circle time. Melissa and Doug and IKEA make small carpets for good prices to simulate this in your home.

A BULLETIN BOARD

The bulletin board is for your use as the teacher to display the calendar and the month's focus on letters, shapes and numbers. You want these visual cues up in your classroom all the time if possible. If the cork board bothers you to have up in your house all the time, you could just put it up during preschool instruction time, but I would encourage you to leave it up as much as possible as part of the immersive learning experience. You should be able to find a cork board about 24" x 36" at office supply stores or stores like Target.

You will also want a place to display your child's art projects. This can be another bulletin board, the refrigerator, a picture ledge or a curtain wire. I use the Dignitet curtain wire from IKEA because it holds projects away from the wall so they can hang up to dry. Regardless of the method you choose, it is helpful for your child's learning and confidence that you display her art projects and calendar board in your "classroom." This is an experience your child would have at a traditional preschool and provides a sense of ownership and important visual cues and reminders of the month's themes and lessons.

CHILD-SIZED TABLE AND CHAIRS

When your child gets to kindergarten he will be expected to sit at a table and work. It is important that he practice sitting at a small table in a chair sized just for him at home, even if it is only for a brief period of time. You may want to consider making a nametag for the back of your child's chair to help with name recognition. If possible, get at least two chairs that look the same so that your child needs to read her name to know which chair is hers. You will also sit at this table with your child so make sure you like it! IKEA has great child-sized furniture for a reasonable price.

Most lessons include opportunities for creative exploration.

ART SUPPLIES

Most lessons include opportunities for creative exploration. For these you will need a variety of art materials including: construction paper, child-sized scissors, markers, crayons, glue, glue sticks, tape, tempera paint, sequins, googly eyes, feathers, coffee filters, liquid watercolor paint or food coloring, a child-sized smock, glitter, stickers, chalk, craft feathers, craft sticks, eye droppers, pencils, golf-sized pencils, watercolor paints, and paint brushes.

Discount School Supply (www.discountschoolsupply.com) is a great online resource for these items with an in-house value line called Colorations. In fact, you can order the Mega Craft Kit from Discount School Supply and it will include most of the materials above to get you started. Ordering your supplies online is generally significantly cheaper than buying craft items locally in-store, but that is also a good option if you need to do it that way.

GOOD TO HAVE
Our Materials and Supplies Checklist (page 43) includes basic supplies and toys that are good to have (but not strictly necessary) throughout the year. You may find notes about where to find specific toys in the curriculum when they come up, but for the most part you can source these materials wherever you want. Melissa and Doug, IKEA, Learning Resources, Lakeshore, and Discount School Supply are all great places to start looking for quality, educational toys at fair prices.

SPECIALTY ITEMS
The list of specialty items includes toys and educational materials that are great to have, but you don't need them right away. You may want to wait until the item comes up in the curriculum and then decide if you want to invest in it. You may decide you don't need the specialty items until your child is older or until she shows special interest in the corresponding subject matter.

You may want to wait until the item comes up in the curriculum and then decide if you want to invest in it.

MATERIALS AND SUPPLIES CHECKLIST

You do not need a slew of specialized items in order to teach The Block Plan Preschool curriculum, it is specifically designed to utilize primarily materials you have in your home already. However, below I have provided a list of useful materials, toys and supplies that will help with activities if you decide you want to purchase them.

LEARNING RESOURCES

Books
Calendar
Zoo-Phonics Small Animal
    Alphabet Cards
Zoo-Phonics Zoo-Coloring
    Book "a-z" (optional)
Handwriting Without Tears:
    Letters and Numbers For
    Me
Music

GOOD TO HAVE: TOYS

Sandbox, Sensory Table or
    Large Tub
Dollhouse
Barn or Farm
Workbench
Play Kitchen
Puzzles
Car Carpet
Trucks and Cars
Magnetic Trains
Animal Planet-Style Animals
    (Safari, Farm, Forest,
    Ocean, Dinosaurs)
Stuffed Animals
Dolls
Dress Up Clothes
Fort-Making Materials
Blocks (Wood, Plastic, Legos
    and/or Foam)
Play Food
Play Pots and Pans
Trowel or Shovel for Digging
Basic Balls (Ball Pit Balls,
Beach Ball and/or
    Playground Ball)

CREATE YOUR SPACE

Hook or Cubby
Carpet or Rug
Bulletin Board
Child-Sized Table & Chairs

ART SUPPLIES

Mega Craft Kit or:
    Construction Paper
    Felt
    Pipe Cleaners
    Googly Eyes
    Feathers
    Pom poms
    Sequins
    Craft sticks
    Beads
    Buttons
    Seashells
    Foam Shapes
    Glitter
    Tissue Paper
    Craft Sand
Watercolor Paints
Dot Art Markers
#2 Pencils
Tempera Paint
Paint Brushes
Markers
Crayons
Child-Sized Scissors
White School Glue
Glue Sticks

GOOD TO HAVE: BASICS

Masking Tape
Hole Punch
Art Smock
Easel
Copy Machine or Printer
Paper Roll
Cotton Balls
Paper Plates
Lunch Bags
Plastic Cups
Stapler
Plastic Eyedroppers

SPECIALTY ITEMS

Unifix Cubes
Magnet Set
Handheld Magnifier
Plastic Tweezers
Bug Jars
Bug Net
Play Insects
Caterpillar to Butterfly
    Habitat
Live Caterpillars
Wisconsin Fast Plants
    Seeds
Musical Instruments
Doctor or Vet Kit
Lacing Cards
Glow-In-The-Dark Star
    Stickers
Kite
Dry Erase Lap Board

SUGGESTED TOY ROTATIONS

"Other old companies, such as Playskool and Fisher-Price, which had built trusted clientele around well-tested toys for small children, succumbed to the control of bigger corporations. Playskool and Fisher-Price specialized in so-called educational playthings. They offered age-appropriate toys, designed and approved by experts in child development. They advertised, if at all, in adult publications like *Parents' Magazine* and stressed that their toys were safe and prepared children for school. **Their toys were largely free of novelty. Gradually, however, these companies abandoned this idealism.** Finally, Playskool was taken over in 1984 by Hasbro and Fisher-Price in 1993 by Mattel, companies whose success has been in novelty toys. **Old-style educational toys survive in the upscale children's and hobby shops where plain blocks and challenging craft sets still can be found. But they are not featured in the discount stores or warehouse toy marts where most toys are purchased."**

— Gary Cross,
Kids' Stuff: Toys and the Changing World of American Childhood

Unfortunately you probably have witnessed exactly this: the cheap, offensively gendered novelty toys are widely available in local toy stores and the quality, basic toys are mostly available online from expensive retailers. Don't let the prevalence of the big box novelty toys deter you from creating an educational world at home for your child. Your house does not need to be full of plastic, noise-making, gendered toys in order for it to be fun for your child.

Many toy companies create toys based on what our children are attracted to and will beg us for, not on what they need or what is good for them. It's our job as parents to provide toys that create opportunities for creativity and exploration. This doesn't necessarily mean toys must be made of wood or be colorless or dull, but neither do they need to be flashy or fancy. In order to engage imagination simple generally is better, and if the toys fit into the goals and themes of your Block Plan Preschool curriculum all the better.

We have a responsibility as parents to find a balance between participating in popular culture and protecting our children from the parts of it that do more harm than good.

As Gary Cross writes, "The progressive legacy of protecting the young from premature entry into the labor market needs now to extended to include the consumer market...Surely we need to go beyond the dichotomous language of austerity versus indulgence. The realistic approach is to be critical participants in our own consumer world, for it is a realm that children live in too. Adults must develop the skills to raise independent children in, rather than against, a culture of consumption." The balance that is right for your family is unique to you. In my family, for example, we watch TV, but only on services like Amazon Instant Video where there are no commercials. We buy new toys, but only for Christmas and birthdays (so no trips to the toy department in Wal-mart).

So how do you know which toys to choose?

I believe the best way to determine the value of a specific toy is to watch how your child plays with it. Does he use any of the following skills with the toy?
- Dramatic play, pretending and creating stories
- Fine or large motor skills
- Manipulative, using skills like sorting or stacking
- Creativity, making up new ways to use the toy or experimenting with what it can do

If the toy doesn't inspire your child to do any of those things maybe it's not the best thing to keep around. (This goes for TV and computer games too, watch how your child uses it to determine value.) I hereby give you permission to give away, donate or throw away any toy that is broken or does not promote good experiences for your child no matter who gave it to you!

Wondering where to shop?

Try Melissa and Doug, IKEA, Land of Nod, Discount School Supply, Learning Resources, Lakeshore and online retailers. If you go into a big box discount store go directly to choose a specific product and try not to linger among the shelves to avoid your child asking for toys you don't want to buy.

In my house we rotate toys meaning I set out toys in the main part of the house that go with our curriculum theme for the month and the rest live in bins in the basement. By keeping most toys in storage at any given time, it keeps the ones we have interesting and fresh so we don't have to buy new ones as often. The result is reduced clutter and a more organized cleaning up process because everything has its place (at least for the month).

Cleaning Up

Have you ever noticed that kids do a lot better with clean up time when they know where something goes? In my first preschool classroom I was disorganized, frankly. I didn't really have designated places for things except in a bin, any bin. Under this "system" clean up time was a disaster and my least favorite part of the day. After awhile my school director came in and helped me sort toys into bins by category (dollhouse dolls in one bin, toy cars in another). I never got organized enough to label the bins (with words for older kids or a photo for non-readers), but this is a common and effective practice in preschools.

My director and I threw away broken toys and pieces that didn't go with anything and reduced the amount of stuff in the classroom by about one third. The effect was amazing. Suddenly cleaning up became a fun sorting game (an early math skill!) and I no longer dreaded it. I didn't have to force the kids to help and started to understand that they didn't help previously because they didn't know where anything belonged. Now I do the same thing in my own house, every toy has a purpose and a designated resting place (for the most part) and everything else is stored in the basement.

A Note About Birthday Parties

While practicing generosity and gift-giving is wonderful, I generally don't like giving toys as birthday party gifts. If you agree, try giving something edible or disposable that doesn't require permanent space in someone's home like stickers, glow sticks or a homemade treat. Books and puzzles also make great gifts because they are so easy to store and donate when you accumulate too many!

Many of my friends have started doing "playdate birthday parties," which are informal gatherings at a park or indoor playground and don't require gifts. If you don't want to go to these parties empty-handed, try helping your child make a painting or free art project that you can turn into a birthday "card." For my son's second birthday I texted his friends' moms in advance and invited them to play with us at his favorite park. It was fun and my son loved playing with his friends, but the day didn't require anything over-the-top or a large monetary investment from anyone.

Time with family and friends is the best part of any holiday anyway!

Now before you start thinking my house is perfect, let me assure you it is not. My house is messy as all homes with young children are and probably should be, but it would be worse if I didn't rotate toys. In the following section are the toy rotations I use that correlate with our monthly themes in the curriculum, I hope they inspire you to devise a toy management strategy that works for your family and enhances the creative life of your child.

If you only allow your child to engage in supervised, adult-led play he won't have a chance to exercise those executive functions of making plans and solving problems on his own.

Free Play
One of the most important things you can do for your child in early childhood is provide plenty of time for free play. Free play is unstructured time when your child can do, basically, whatever she wants. Research by Sergio and Vivien Pellis detailed in "The Function of Play in the Development of the Social Brain" suggests that play during childhood changes the structure of the prefrontal cortex in the human brain in a way that increases social skills. The prefrontal cortex is responsible for regulating emotions, making plans and solving problems, which is why free play is so essential to the make changes in the brain. If you only allow your child to engage in supervised, adult-led play he won't have a chance to exercise those executive functions of making plans and solving problem on his own.

Ideally, with the help of The Block Plan Preschool curriculum and suggested toys, you will create a stimulating environment at home for your child that encourages creativity both indoors and out, and then you will be able to let your child play alone for awhile each day.

The balance of both types of play, free play and engagement with you, are optimal for your child's development and education. The Block Plan Preschool is designed to create space in your family life for both types of play to maximize benefit for your child.

SUGGESTED TOY ROTATIONS

Below is a brief summary of the themes for each month of curriculum, you can use this as a reference for organizing toys in your home. For more comprehensive lists see the title pages of each month of curriculum.

September
Red, Circle, Cars, Truck & Trains, Rolling, Rocks & Balance

October
Orange, Triangle, Fall, Books, Cutting

November
Brown, Square, Family, Mountains, Cooking

December
Green, Star, Holidays, Music, Art, Dancing, Magnets

January
White, Rectangle, Dinosaurs, Sports, Snow, Cold

February
Pink, Heart, Human Body, Five Senses, Sliding, Pets

March
Purple, Diamond, Farm, Nature, Digging

April
Blue, Oval, Oceans, Ponds, Swimming

May
Yellow, Animals, Insects, Rain Forest, All About Me

SEPTEMBER
Dramatic Play: Dollhouse (With Firehouse Characters if Desired)
Carpet: Road
Puzzles: Transportation
Thematic: Cars, Trucks, Dump Truck, Fire Truck, Magnetic Train
Manipulative: Marbles (Warning: Choking Hazard)
Large Motor: Indoor Strider Bike or Riding Toy
Sensory: IncredibleFoam
Block Set: Legos with Ramps (Choose a Size Appropriate for Your Child's Age)

OCTOBER
Dramatic Play: Workbench
Carpet: Road
Puzzles: Outer Space, Forest
Thematic: Pumpkins, Space Ship, Stars
Dress-Up Clothes, Forest Animals
Manipulative: Ice Cube Tray Marked with Colors & Pom Poms for Sorting
Large Motor: Fort-Making Materials
Sensory: Water Marbles
Blocks: Wooden

NOVEMBER
Dramatic Play: Kitchen
Carpet: Sheepskin
Puzzles: Food, Alphabet
Thematic: Play Food, Pots and Pans, Play Dough, Teddy Bears, Wind Ribbons
Manipulative: Counting Bears
Large Motor: Floor Tiles (Made of Carpet Pieces or Marked with Numbers)
Sensory: Dried Beans
Blocks: Foam

DECEMBER

Dramatic Play: Farm (With Nativity Characters If Desired)
Carpet: Sheepskin
Puzzles: Felt Tree, Numbers
Thematic: Drum, Piano, Instruments, Ribbons and Scarves for Dance, Farm Animals
Manipulative: Magnets
Large Motor: Indoor Corn Hole Bean Bag Game
Sensory: Wrapping Paper for Tearing or Cutting
Blocks: Legos (Choose Appropriate Size)

JANUARY

Dramatic Play: Workbench
Carpet: Dinosaur
Puzzles: Dinosaurs, Sports
Thematic: Winter Clothes Dress Up, Dinosaurs, Sled, Sports Equipment (Soccer Balls, Golf Clubs, etc.)
Manipulative: 2x4 with Nails Sunk Halfway, Used For Sorting Washers & Nuts
Large Motor: Indoor Sled or Spinning Toy
Sensory: Cotton Balls
Blocks: Wooden

FEBRUARY

Dramatic Play: Dollhouse
Carpet: Road
Puzzles: Pets
Thematic: Stuffed Animals, Dolls, Doll Bed & Bath, Small Blankets, Doctor or Vet Kit
Manipulative: Unifix Cubes
Large Motor: Indoor Riding Toy
Sensory: Pieces of Burlap or Sand Paper
Blocks: Legos (Choose Appropriate Size)

MARCH

Dramatic Play: Farm
Carpet: Numbers
Puzzles: Farm
Thematic: Farm Animals, Barn, Pots and "Dirt," Gardening Tools
Manipulative: Ice Cube Tray with Seeds For Sorting
Large Motor: Bouncing Toy Like Benny the Bull or Trampoline
Sensory: Dried Corn or Rice
Blocks: Wooden

APRIL

Dramatic Play: Kitchen
Carpet: Blue Ocean
Puzzles: Sea Life and Ocean
Thematic: Ocean Animals, Swim Dress Up, Sand Toys, Ball Pit
Manipulative: Easter Eggs and Pom Poms
Large Motor: Ball Pit in a Plastic Play Pool
Sensory: Water Table
Blocks: Foam

MAY

Dramatic Play: Workbench
Carpet: Numbers
Puzzles: Safari, Insects
Thematic: Safari Animals, Toy Insects, Bug Jars and Nets, Magnifying Glass, Summer Clothes Dress Up
Manipulative: Plastic Insects
Large Motor: Play Lawn Mower
Sensory: Play Dough
Blocks: Legos (Choose Appropriate Size)

CONNECTING WITH OTHER BLOCK PLAN PRESCHOOL FAMILIES

"A less direct form of parental peer pressure occurs when other parents put their children in organized sports programs so that there are no longer any children in the neighborhood who are available for free play or just hanging out... One option is to find other parents who feel as you do and arrange for your children to play together."

– David Elkind, *The Hurried Child*

So you've made the decision to simplify your life, use The Block Plan Preschool curriculum at home and keep your child out of expensive, organized programs. What do you do when it feels like everyone around you is putting their children into programs outside the home? What if you feel like you're the only one doing it differently? What if your child is having a hard time making friends because there is no one around in your neighborhood? The answer is: connect with other families who are doing the same thing as you are.

On these pages are some ideas about how to find other Block Plan Preschool families in your area, what you can do together and how you can find support when you need it. Life, after all, is a social experience and the connections we make in our community are important, I just don't believe you should have to pay to join an activity in order to make friends.

Form a Group

Do you have friends who have a similar approach to early childhood with their children? Start your own group! It doesn't need to be formal or big, just choose a place and a time and agree to meet as often as works for you.

I host a group at my house once a month for four friends and their kids. It's a super casual, come-if-you-can arrangement and helps us all feel so much more connected and supported as parents and friends. It's also very easy for our kids to play together because we all use The Block Plan Preschool and have a similar approach to parenting. If this sounds good to you I encourage you to try it!

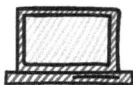

Read the Melissa and Doug Blog

The Melissa and Doug toy company has started a movement called Take Back Childhood and they publish wonderful blog posts about it on their website www. melissaanddoug.com. Visit their blog to read about Melissa's ideas for learning through play and how other families balance free play and learning.

Connect with The Block Plan Preschool on Social Media

The Block Plan Preschool website and Facebook page are places you can go to get new information and support as you work through the curriculum at home. We will post updates about great ideas, toys and products that can help support your child's learning at home. If you want to share stories or photos about how you are making the program work and are pursuing a healthy, active and creative life for your children please let us know or post on our Facebook page!

Support the Mission

I hope you will talk to parents, grandparents, at-home child care providers and pre-school teachers you know about The Block Plan Preschool. My overall mission is to help affect change in how we approach early childhood education in the United States by empowering parents to take an active role in their child's education.

The Block Plan Preschool is a way to bring families closer together and preserve the parts of healthy childhood that are in danger of fading away in our current technolog-ical and social climate. I hope you will feel as inspired by your work at home with your child as I do and will share the story of this program with others!

As more families start teaching their children The Block Plan Preschool way, there will be more support available for you and for your family's way of life. The ultimate goal is to make learning through play, spending fun free time together as a family, and educating your kids in this way not so counter-cultural but normal things to do. When that happens it will benefit us all!

CURRICULUM OVERVIEW

"You can teach a student a lesson for a day; but if you can teach him to learn by creating curiosity he will continue the learning process as long as he lives."

– Clay P. Bedford,
Former Business Executive

This is an overview of the curriculum contained in *The Block Plan Preschool: Preparing Your Child at Home for Kindergarten*. The curriculum is how you will teach your child about his world, introduce him to a life of learning, and help him build strong, fulfilling relationships within your family. While the lessons are important, the highest priority is to cultivate a sense of curiosity in your child so that she will always see learning as a fun and exciting adventure. Don't worry about pushing too hard or following perceived rules, go the direction your child wants to go and have fun alongside her. Your years in The Block Plan Preschool will be a grand adventure!

If this handbook was given to you by a preschool or at-home child care provider, the curriculum overview will give you an idea of what your child is learning each month in school so you can support her learning at home.

If this handbook was given to you by parents and you are a grandparent then the overview may give you some ideas about what you can do with your grandchildren that will complement their learning at home.

If you are a new parent and someone has given you this book as a gift or if you found it on your own as a place to begin, the curriculum overview will give you an idea of how to start shaping your home environment to stimulate your child's curiosity and understanding from the earliest years.

Regardless of how you ended up here, you are very welcome! Learning happens in all areas of a child's life and it's to his benefit that everyone is on the same page. Enjoy!

SEPTEMBER

Welcome to a new year of preschool! September is a wonderful time of new discovery, excitement and change. You will guide your child as she gets used to a new daily routine with possibly a little more structure than she had over the summer. This begins a new season of challenge, stretching, growing, excitement, interest and discovery. Below are your focuses for the month including letters, numbers, a color, a shape and various themes that will all tie in and work together throughout this month of curriculum.

In September your preschooler's world is on the move! Kids in the neighborhood are riding bikes and buses to school, road construction is underway, and trash trucks are driving down the street! We'll begin the curriculum by exploring all this action by learning about things that go, circles and the wheels that keep us rolling. We will play with rolling toys, experiment with balance and rolling objects, and practice riding a bike. We will review fire safety and learn not to be afraid of firefighters. We will introduce print awareness, counting, shape awareness, and practice writing numbers zero and one. Enjoy, and welcome to the Block Plan Preschool!

Tt, Rr, Kk
0, 1
Red
Circle
Back to School
Cars, Trucks & Trains
Transportation
Rocks & Balance
Kindness
Respect
Fire Safety
Sensory: Rolling
Motor Skills: Riding a Bike

SEPTEMBER BOOK LIST

One-time purchase used all year:
- Zoo-phonics Small Animal Alphabet Cards
- Handwriting Without Tears: Letters and Numbers for Me workbook (for the 4- and 5-year-old years, consider making copies so you can use it multiple years)
- "Kids in Action" by Greg & Steve
- "Kids in Motion" by Greg & Steve

Week 1
- *Pledge of Allegiance* (Scholastic, 2000)
- *Shapes That Roll* (Nagel)
- *This is the Way We Go To School* (Baer)
- **Wemberly Worried* (Henkes)
- *A Life Like Mine* (DK Printing and Unicef) – Section: Development
- *At the Firehouse* (Rockwell)
- ***Firefighters to the Rescue Around the World* (Staniford)
- ***Scholastic First Picture Dictionary* (Scholastic, 2009) – Section: "In the city"

Week 2
- **I Stink!* (McMullan) or *I'm Dirty!* (McMullan)
- *When I Build With Blocks* (Alling) or *Dreaming Up: A Celebration of Building* (Hale)
- **Sheep in a Jeep* (Shaw)
- *The Little Engine That Could* (Piper)
- *The Wheels on the School Bus* (Moore)
- *What Do Wheels Do All Day?* (Prince)
- ***Hide and Seek: Things That Go* (Sirett)
- ***Mike Mulligan and His Steam Shovel* (Burton)

Week 3
- *Mufaro's Beautiful Daughters* (Steptoe)
- *Balancing Act* (Walsh)
- **Five Little Monkeys* (Christelow)
- *Curious George* (Rey)
- *Sally Jean the Bicycle Queen* (Best) or *Duck on a Bike* (Shannon)
- ***Red Truck* (Hamilton)
- ***Little Blue Truck* (Schertle)
- "The Balancing Act" from "Kids in Motion" (song)
- "Beanie Bag Dance" from "Kids in Action" (song)

Week 4
- *Clifford the Big Red Dog* (Bridwell)
- *My First Airplane Ride* (Hubbell)
- ***The Lost (and Found) Balloon* (Jenkins)
- ***The Noon Balloon* (Brown)

Key
* = Book used in literacy lesson
** = Book used in extra lessons

September Focus Page

🖨 Copy on red paper

✂ Cut out shapes & mount on white paper

🪄 Laminate for durability

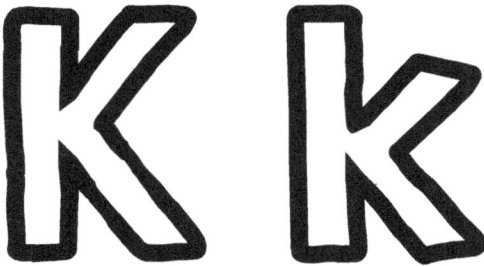

T t R r
K k
I O ◯

BPP0912

The Block Plan Preschool, BPP0912

OCTOBER

Welcome to the official beginning of fall! This month you will explore changing seasons, holiday traditions, classic children's literature, nursery rhymes, the night sky, and the joy of reading with your child! All the lessons and adventures this month tie into the feeling of transition that is part of October: orange is a secondary color between red and yellow, fall is a season caught between cold and hot, and early childhood is an age between babyhood and childhood. This curriculum will help you and your child settle into and enjoy this transitional time by opening your eyes to the changing fall forest, practicing patience, feeling squishy pumpkins and exercising your bodies by climbing high!

Oo, Hh
2, 3
Orange
Triangle
Halloween
Fall
Color Mixing
Gravity & Outer Space
Books
Patience
Road Safety
Sensory: Squishy
Motor Skills: Climbing & Cutting

OCTOBER BOOK LIST

Week 1

- *The Hat* (Brett)
- *Gravity* (Chin)
- *There Was an Old Lady Who Swallowed a Fly* (Colandro)
- *Olivia* (Falconer)
- *The Reasons for Seasons* (Gibbons)
- *Lola at the Library* (McQuinn)
- **It's Fall!* (Glaser)
- ***Scholastic First Picture Dictionary* (Scholastic, 2009) – Section: "In the house"
- "Animal Action I" from "Kids in Motion" (song)

Week 2

- *The Itsy Bitsy Spider* (Trapani)
- *Leo the Late Bloomer* (Krauss)
- *I Ain't Gonna Paint No More* (Beaumont)
- *Mouse Paint* (Walsh)
- *Time to Sleep* (Fleming)
- *The Royal Treasure Measure* (Harris)
- *Buster Climbs the Walls* (Brown)
- ***Forest Bright, Forest Night* (Ward)
- ***Ruby in Her Own Time* (Emmett)
- "Bop 'Til You Drop" from "Kids in Action" (song)
- "The Freeze" from "Kids in Motion" (song)

Week 3

- *The Carrot Seed* (Krauss)
- *Measure It (Tool Kit)* (Whitehouse)
- *The Three Little Pigs* (Marshall)
- *The Little Old Lady Who Was Not Afraid of Anything* (Williams)
- *Pumpkins* (Robbins)
- *Humpty Dumpty* (Kubler) or *Humpty Dumpty* (Kirk)
- *Sam and the Tigers* (Lester)
- ***My First Mother Goose* (dePaola) *or Mother Goose* (Grant)
- ***Kitten's First Full Moon* (Henkes)
- "Animal Action II" from "Kids in Motion" (song)

Week 4

- *The Three Bears Halloween* (Duval) or *Space Case* (Marshall)
- *A Day With Police Officers* (Shepherd)
- ***Goodnight Moon* (Brown)
- ***Frederick* (Lionni)

Key

* = Book used in literacy lesson
** = Book used in extra lessons

October Focus Page

🖨 Copy on orange paper

✂️ Cut out shapes & mount on white paper

🪄 Laminate for durability

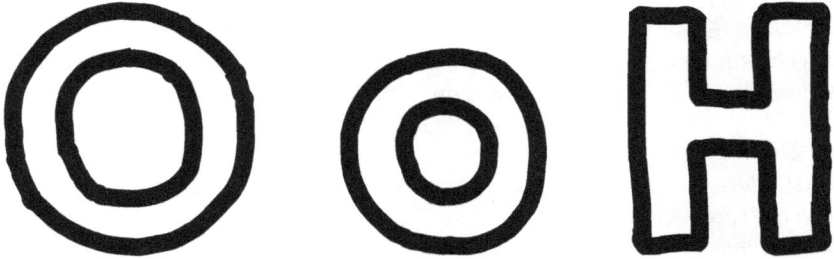

O o H

h 2

3

The Block Plan Preschool, BPP1011

NOVEMBER

November is the beginning of the holiday season! As the weather turns colder we turn our attentions inward to focus on being grateful for what we have, the family around us no matter what form that family takes, and baking and cooking for people we love! This month we will notice all the brown around us and read many stories about brown bears. We will learn about squares, which have four sides, and feel the crunchy brown leaves that fall on the ground. We will practice scooping and stirring in our cooking science lessons and learn about the windy weather that blows the leaves and makes the bears know it's time to hibernate. We will talk about being a good guest and how to recognize tricky people so we can keep ourselves safe. We will practice gratefulness and prepare our hearts and kitchens for Thanksgiving!

Nn, Bb, Ss
4
Brown
Square
Thanksgiving
Family
Weather
Mountains
Gratefulness
Tricky People Safety
Sensory: Crunchy
Motor Skills: Scooping & Stirring

NOVEMBER BOOK LIST

Week 1
- *We're Going on a Bear Hunt (Rosen)
- Gilberto and the Wind (Ets)
- Sally Goes to the Mountains (Huneck)
- My Trip to the Mountains (Harder) or Mountains (Hutmacher)
- Big Mama (Crunk)
- **Tikki Tikki Tembo (Mosel)
- **Scholastic First Picture Dictionary (Scholastic, 2009) – Section: "In the mountains"
- "Going On a Bear Hunt" from "Kids in Action" (song)

Week 2
- *Goldilocks and the Three Bears (Marshall)
- How to Babysit a Grandpa (Reagan) and/or How to Babysit a Grandma (Reagan)
- *Jamberry (Degen)
- What Aunts Do Best/What Uncles Do Best (Numeroff) or Brothers and Sisters (Read)
- Silly Sally (Wood)
- The Wind Blew (Hutchins)
- **Are You My Mother? (Eastman)
- **If You Give a Mouse a Cookie (Numeroff)
- "The Freeze" from "Kids in Motion" or "Rock 'n Stop" by Eric Chappelle (songs)
- "Beanie Bag Dance" from "Kids in Action" (song)

Week 3
- The Tale of Rabbit and Coyote (Johnston)
- Thanksgiving is for Giving Thanks (Sutherland)
- *Jesse Bear, What Will You Wear? (Carlstrom)
- Tattered Sails (Kay)
- The Little Mouse, the Red Ripe Strawberry, and the Big Hungry Bear (Wood)
- **Pilgrim Children Had Many Chores (Lem-Tardif)
- **Jonathan and His Mommy (Smalls)
- "Bop 'Til You Drop" from "Kids in Action" (song)

Week 4
- Brown Bear, Brown Bear, What Do You See? (Martin)
- The First Thanksgiving Day: A Counting Story (Melmed)
- **The Story of Thanksgiving (Skarmeas)
- **The Runaway Bunny (Brown)

Key
* = Book used in literacy lesson
** = Book used in extra lessons

November Focus Page

Copy on brown paper

Cut out shapes & mount on white paper

Laminate for durability

N B S

b

4 n s

BPP1111

The Block Plan Preschool, BPP1111

DECEMBER

December is a season of contrasts, we simultaneously experience and hold within us peace and excitement, darkness and lights, music and quiet, solitude and crowds, dancing and stillness. This month we will learn about the number five and the star with five points. We will study Hannukah and Christmas and religions around the world that celebrate all different types of holidays! We will learn to respect differences and embrace traditions practiced by our own families. December's pull is like the magnet, sometimes it feels that we are moving toward it all year long! Then we are released as the winter solstice passes and we move on to a bright new year. This curriculum will help your child manage the excitement of this special season and disperse the focus from gifts and impatience to art, music, performance, peace and traditions that make this dark time of year so special for us all!

Dd, Gg, Pp
5
Green
Star
Christmas, Hanukkah, Winter Holidays
Music
Art
Magnets
Lights
Peace
Crowd Safety
Sensory: Soft
Motor Skills: Dancing

DECEMBER BOOK LIST

Week 1
- *The Story of Ferdinand* (Leaf)
- *The Story of Hanukkah* (Adler)
- **Rosie's Walk* (Hutchins)
- *Magnets: Pulling Together, Pushing Apart* (Rosinsky)
- *Angelina Ballerina* (Holabird)
- ***In the Garden with Van Gogh* (Merberg)
- ***Scholastic First Picture Dictionary* (Scholastic, 2009) – Section: "In the grocery store"

Week 2
- **Go Away Big Green Monster* (Emberley)
- *Go Dog Go* (Eastman)
- *Museum ABC* (The [NY] Metropolitan Museum of Art)
- *Giraffes Can't Dance* (Andreae)
- **Where Is the Green Sheep?* (Fox)
- *A Life Like Mine* (DK Printing and Unicef) – Section: Participation
- ***A Little Peace* (Kerley)
- ***Magnets (All Aboard Science Reader)* (Schreiber)
- "Rock 'n Stop" by Eric Chappelle (song)
- "Beanie Bag Dance" from "Kids in Action" (song)
- "Bee Beat" by Eric Chappelle, "The Nutcracker" by Tchaikovsky, "Baby Einstein: Traveling Melodies", or other music to inspire creative dance! (songs)

Week 3
- **Wiggle* (Cronin)
- *Miss Rumphius* (Cooney)
- *Barn Dance* (Martin)
- *The Shortest Day: Celebrating the Winter Solstice* (Pfeffer)
- *The Story of Christmas* (Pingry)
- ***Light the Lights: A Story About Celebrating Hanukkah and Christmas* (Moorman)
- ***Child's Book of Art* (Micklethwait)
- "Balancing Act" from "Kids in Motion" (song)
- "Silent Night" and other holiday music from any professional recording you like

Week 4
- *Corduroy* (Freeman)
- *The Night Before Christmas* (Moore, Hobbie)
- ***Kwanzaa* (Schaefer)
- ***Painting with Picasso* (Merberg)

Key
* = Book used in literacy lesson
** = Book used in extra lessons

December Focus Page

🖨 Copy on green paper

✂ Cut out shapes & mount on white paper

✨ Laminate for durability

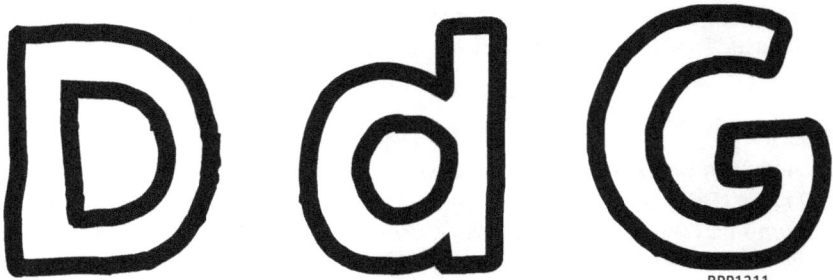

BPP1211

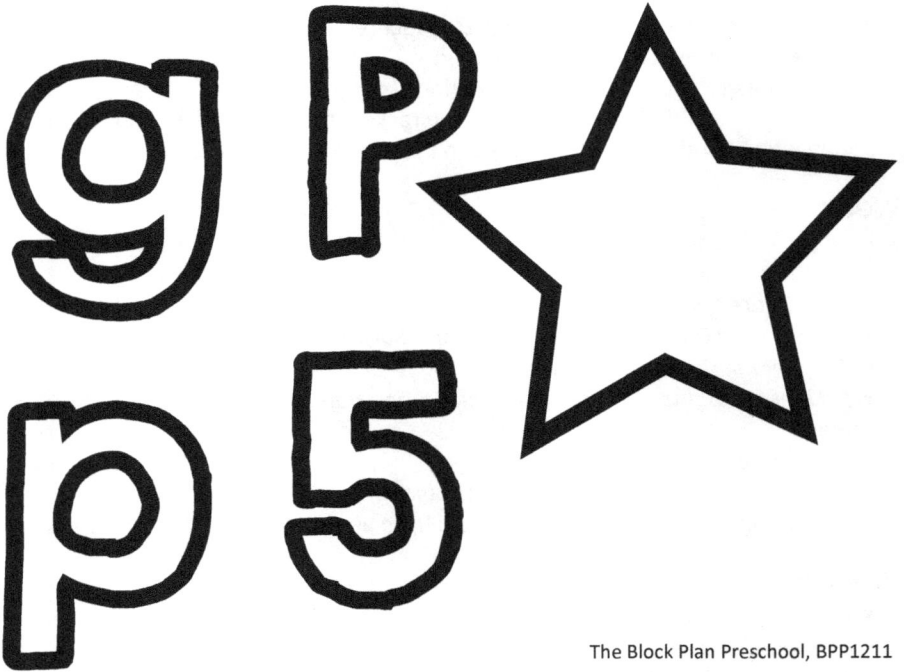

The Block Plan Preschool, BPP1211

JANUARY

Brrrrr, January is all about the cold! Cold weather safety, feeling cold sensations on your skin, preventing colds, snowmen who live in the cold! We will learn about dinosaurs and take a trip to a science and nature museum to see dinosaur bones and practice self-regulation (managing your emotions and behaviors and following rules). We'll learn about rectangles and sports, especially baseball, football and soccer, which are the simplest for young children to play. We will practice the important gross motor skills of throwing, catching and kicking a ball just like they do in games like the Super Bowl! We will learn about Martin Luther King, Jr. and talk about how all people are different, but all are special and important. We will also make a New Year's resolution and recommit ourselves to the special time of learning and growing together during early childhood!

**Jj, Ww, Cc
6
White
Rectangle
The New Year
Dinosaurs
Sports
Snow and Cold
Self-Regulation
Cold Safety
Sensory: Cold
Motor Skills: Throwing, Catching &
Kicking a Ball**

JANUARY BOOK LIST

Week 1
- *Squirrel's New Year's Resolution* (Miller)
- *New Year's Day* (Peppas)
- **Where the Wild Things Are* (Sendak)
- *I Dreamt I Was a Dinosaur* (Blackstone)
- *Dinosaurs, Dinosaurs* (Barton) or *How the Dinosaur Got to the Museum* (Hartland)
- ***My Big Dinosaur Book* (Priddy)
- ***Saturday Night at the Dinosaur Stomp* (Shields)
- ***Strega Nona* (DePaola)
- "Beanie Bag Dance" from "Kids in Action" (song)

Week 2
- **Snowballs* (Ehlert)
- *Snowmen at Night (Buehner)*
- **The Flea's Sneeze* (Downey)
- *The Jacket I Wear in the Snow* (Neitzel) or *Thomas' Snowsuit* (Munsch)
- *No, David!* (Shannon)
- *Stone Soup* (Forest)
- ***The First Snowfall* (Rockwell)
- ***Cloudy with a Chance of Meatballs* (Barrett)
- "Going On a Bear Hunt" and "Bop 'Til You Drop" from "Kids in Action" (songs)
- "The Freeze" from "Kids in Motion" (song)

Week 3
- **The Snowy Day* (Keats)
- *The Crayon Box That Talked* (Derolf)
- *I am Martin Luther King, Jr.* (Meltzer)
- *Joy in Mudville* (Raczka)
- *Which Sport Will I Play Today?* (Harder) or *DK Eyewitness Books: Sports* (Hammond)
- *How Do Dinosaurs Play with Their Friends?* (Yolen)
- ***Goodnight Football* (Dahl)
- ***Let's Talk Soccer* (Falk)
- "Free to Be You and Me" by Marlo Thomas (song)
- "Animal Action II" from "Kids in Motion" (song)

Week 4
- *Snow* (Shulevitz)
- *The Little Snowplow* (Koehler)
- ***Bartholomew and the Oobleck* (Seuss)
- ***The Great Animal Search* (Young)

Key
* = Book used in literacy lesson
** = Book used in extra lessons

January Focus Page

Copy on white paper

Cut out shapes & mount on black or gray paper

Laminate for durability

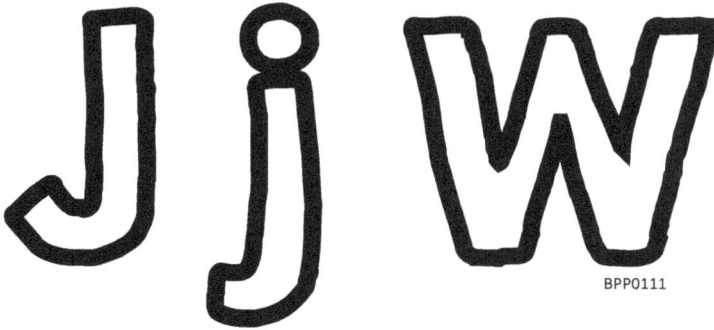

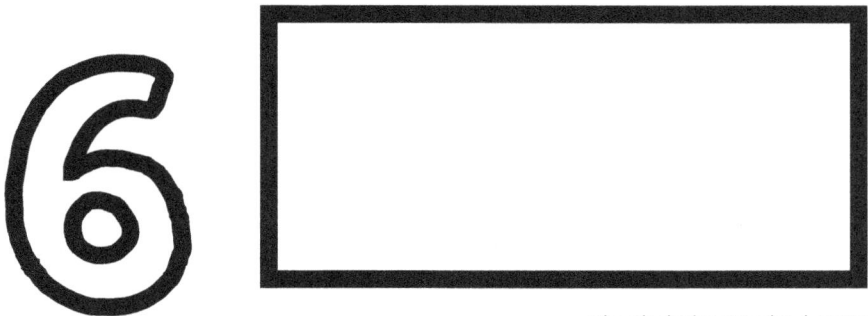

J j W

BPP0111

w C c

6

The Block Plan Preschool, BPP0111

FEBRUARY

In February we focus on humanity: who we are as people, how humans are the same and how they are different, who and how we love, how we treat others and what our bodies can do. We will celebrate Valentine's Day with hearts and the color pink! We will explore the different skin colors, eye colors, hair colors, body types and cultures that make up the world. We will talk about all the different jobs people do, pets that people have and places that people live. We'll feel what it's like to slide either on skis, sleds, skates or all three. We will talk about our feelings and emotional safety, both for ourselves and for others. We will explore emotions like anger, happiness, frustration, excitement and fear and learn ways to cope with them all. We will explore and practice using our five senses: touch, taste, smell, sight and hearing in order to better engage with the world.

Ff, Vv, Qq, Ll
7
Pink
Heart
Valentine's Day
People
Human Body
Five Senses
Pets
Feelings
Love
Generosity
Emotional Safety
Sensory: Rough
Motor Skills: Sliding
(Skiing, Sledding or Skating)

FEBRUARY BOOK LIST

Week 1
- *Fancy Nancy* (O'Connor)
- *The Way I Feel* (Cain) or *The Feelings Book* (Parr)
- *Cookie's Week* (Ward)
- *Today I Feel Silly* (Curtis)
- *What Pet Should I Get?* (Seuss)
- **Pete the Cat: I Love My White Shoes* (Litwin)
- **Busy, Busy Town* (Scarry)
- "Animal Action II" from "Kids in Motion" (song)

Week 2
- *I'll Teach My Dog a Lot of Words* (Frith)
- *When Sophie Gets Angry...Really, Really Angry* (Bang)
- *Bark, George* (Feiffer)
- *We're Different, We're the Same* (Kates)
- *The Day It Rained Hearts* (Bond) or *Valentine's Day* (Rockwell)
- *People* (Spier)
- **Scholastic First Picture Dictionary* (Scholastic, 2009) – Section: "The body"
- **Black is Brown is Tan* (Adoff) or *The Colors of Us* (Katz)
- "Free to Be You and Me" by Marlo Thomas (song)
- "Beanie Bag Dance" from "Kids in Action" (song)
- "Bop 'Til You Drop" from "Kids in Action" (song)

Week 3
- *Louie* (Keats)
- *A Life Like Mine* (DK Printing and Unicef) – Section: "Protection"
- *Is Your Mama a Llama?* (Guarino)
- *Franklin in the Dark* (Bourgeois)
- *My Five Senses* (Aliki)
- **Alexander and the Terrible, Horrible, No Good, Very Bad Day* (Viorst)
- **The Story of Abraham Lincoln* (Pingry) or *The Story of George Washington* (Pingry)
- "We're Going On a Bear Hunt" from "Kids in Action" (song)

Week 4
- *Roar! A Noisy Counting Book* (Edwards)
- *The Quilt Story* (Johnston)
- **Mama, Do You Love Me* (Joosse) and/or *Papa, Do You Love Me* (Joosse)
- **Yoko* (Wells)

Key
* = Book used in literacy lesson
** = Book used in extra lessons

February Focus Page

🖨 Copy on pink paper

✂️ Cut out shapes & mount on white paper

🪄 Laminate for durability

F f V v

Q L ♡

7 q l

BPP0211

The Block Plan Preschool, BPP0211

MARCH

March is the beginning of spring and an awakening from winter! The world is coming alive again with sun and plants working their way back to life. It is time to get outside, explore nature, dig in the soil, learn about growing vegetables and flowers, and prepare to go camping (even if it's only inside for now)! We will learn all about farms, the animals that live there, family gardens, and where our food comes from. We will learn about sun safety, wearing hats and sunscreen, drinking water and taking clothing layers with you outdoors. We will learn about gentle touch and gentleness of spirit. We will practice digging in sand boxes, sensory tables, and garden beds. We will fly kites, go for a nature scavenger hunt and visit a farm! It is time to enjoy the great outdoors with your little explorer!

Mm, Xx, Uu
8
Purple
Diamond
Farm
Nature
Plants & Seeds
Camping
St. Patrick's Day
Gentleness
Sun Safety
Sensory: Food (Dried Corn, Rice, Beans)
Motor Skills: Digging

MARCH BOOK LIST

Week 1
- *Big Red Barn* (Brown)
- *How a Plant Grows* (Kalman) or *From Seed to Plant* (Gibbons)
- **Barnyard Banter* (Fleming)
- *Hands are Not for Hitting* (Agassi) and/or *Teeth are Not for Biting* (Verdick)
- *My First Book About Farms* (Einhorn) or *Over on the Farm* (Gunson)
- **Ten Seeds (Brown)
- ***Scholastic First Picture Dictionary* (Scholastic, 2009) – Section: "On the farm"
- "Beanie Bag Dance" from "Kids in Action" (song)

Week 2
- **Growing Vegetable Soup* (Ehlert)
- *A Fruit is a Suitcase for Seeds* (Hariton)
- *Let's Fly a Kite* (Murphy)
- *Stuck* (Jeffers)
- **Muncha! Muncha! Muncha!* (Fleming)
- *This Year's Garden* (Rylant)
- ***A Garden Alphabet* (Wilner)
- ***Alejandro's Gift* (Albert)
- "Get Outdoors" or "In Love with Nature" by Jeff and Paige (songs)
- "Balancing Act" from "Kids in Motion" (song)

Week 3
- **Planting a Rainbow* (Ehlert)
- *Shapes, Shapes, Shapes* (Hoban)
- *Lifetimes (Rice)*
- *When I Go Camping* (Harder) or *Camping Day* (Lakin)
- *The Empty Pot* (Demi)
- *I Took a Walk* (Cole) or *We're Going on a Nature Hunt* (Metzger)
- ***St. Patrick's Day* (Gibbons)
- ***Scholastic First Picture Dictionary* (Scholastic, 2009) – Section: "Camping"
- "Animal Action II" from "Kids in Motion" (song)

Week 4
- **I Went Walking* (Williams)
- *Harold and the Purple Crayon* (Johnson)
- ***The Shaman's Apprentice* (Cherry and Plotkin)
- ***This is the Sunflower* (Schaefer) or *Dandelions: Stars in the Grass* (Posada)

Key
* = Book used in literacy lesson
** = Book used in extra lessons

March Focus Page

🖨 Copy on purple paper

✂ Cut out shapes & mount on white paper

🪄 Laminate for durability

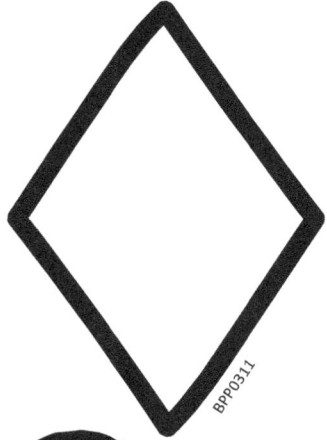

BPP0311

The Block Plan Preschool, BPP0311

APRIL

April is a time of new life! We celebrate spring, hatching baby chicks, Easter, rain showers, and local ponds coming back to life after a long winter! We will do many experiments and exploration with water and bubbles. We will explore the ocean ecosystem and the animals that live there, and learn about how they swim! We will practice swimming and water safety skills to empower our children to manage their own risks in and around water. We will learn what is unique and special about ovals and eggs. We will learn about joy, how to share it and how the other character lessons from this year all contribute to developing lasting joy for our children, ourselves and our families!

Aa, Ee
q
Blue
Oval
Water
Bubbles
Spring
Ocean Animals & Ecosystem
Pond Animals & Ecosystem
Easter
Joy
Water Safety
Sensory: Wet
Motor Skills: Swimming

APRIL BOOK LIST

Week 1

- *Rainbow Fish* (Pfister)
- *Baby Beluga* (Raffi)
- *Commotion in the Ocean* (Andreae)
- **Don't Let the Pigeon Drive the Bus* (Willems)
- *The Pout-Pout Fish* (Diesen)
- *What Floats? What Sinks? A Look at Density* (Boothroyd)
- ***Hello Fish! Visiting the Coral Reef* (Earle) or *Oceans* (Green)
- ***Scholastic First Picture Dictionary* (Scholastic, 2009) – Section: "By the sea"
- "The Freeze" from "Kids in Motion" or "Rock 'n Stop" by Eric Chappelle (songs)

Week 2

- *If You're Happy and You Know It* (Cabrera)
- **Big Fat Hen* (Baker)
- *Pop! A Book About Bubbles* (Bradley)
- *Chicka Chicka Boom Boom* (Martin, Archambault)
- *How To Make Monstrous, Huge, Unbelievably Big Bubbles* (Stein)
- *It's Mine!* (Lionni)
- **The Napping House* (Wood)
- *Sand Castle* (Yee)
- **Easter (Gibbons)
- ***Benny's Big Bubble* (O'Connor)
- "Bop 'Til You Drop" from "Kids in Action" (song)
- "Amphibious" or "Whales" by Eric Chappelle (songs)

Week 3

- **One Duck Stuck* (Root)
- *Life in a Pond* (Hibbert)
- **Splash* (Jonas)
- *The Rain Came Down* (Shannon)
- *Water Can Be* (Salas) or *Water is Water* (Paul)
- ***In the Small, Small Pond* (Fleming)
- ***It's Spring!* (Glaser)
- "Beanie Bag Dance" from "Kids in Action" (song)

Week 4

- **Caps for Sale* (Slobodkina)
- *A Life Like Mine* (DK Printing and Unicef) – Section: "Survival"
- ***All the Water in the World* (Lyon)
- ***Three Little Fish and the Big Bad Shark* (Grace, Geist)

Key

* = Book used in literacy lesson
** = Book used in extra lessons

April Focus Page

Copy on blue paper

Cut out shapes & mount on white paper

Laminate for durability

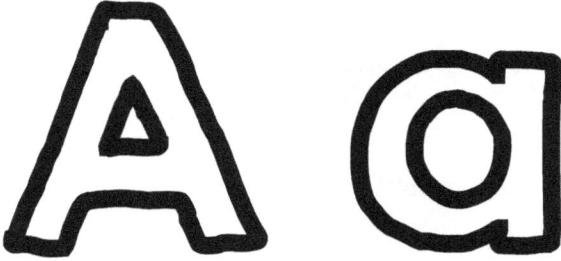

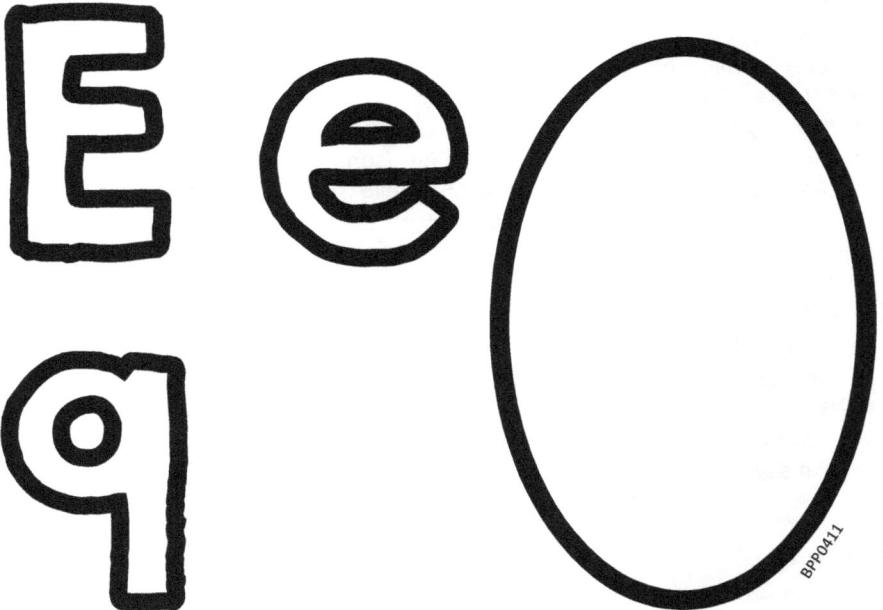

A a

E e O

q

The Block Plan Preschool, BPP0411

MAY

May is our last month of curriculum for the year! Congratulations!
You and your child have both worked hard
learning and playing this year.

In May we will have so much fun learning about animals and insects now that it's warmer outside! We will visit the zoo and learn about animals that live in hot places such as the rain forest, jungle and faraway grasslands. We will learn about heat safety to keep us safe outdoors this summer and how the yellow sun works to create that heat. We will learn about insects you find in the backyard and how a caterpillar transforms into a butterfly! We will run, jump and play with stretchy materials, practice counting to ten and review all the shapes we learned about this year. Your child will practice skills that will help him with kindergarten next year like telling time, lacing shoelaces, making a presentation and accessing his senses of trust and courage.

Thank you for joining us on this learning adventure this year! We
hope you have fun this month and wish you a
playful, relaxing summer break!

Ii, Yy, Zz
10
Yellow
Shapes Review
Animals
Insects
Zoo
Rain Forest
The Sun
All About Me
Trust & Courage
Heat Safety
Sensory: Stretchy
Motor Skills: Running & Jumping

MAY BOOK LIST

Week 1
- *Rumble in the Jungle* (Andreae)
- *A House is a House for Me* (Hoberman)
- **The Grouchy Ladybug* (Carle)
- *It's About Time!* (Murphy)
- *Little Kids First Big Book of Animals* (Hughes)
- *The View at the Zoo* (Bostrom)
- ***Who's Hiding Here?* (Yoshi)
- ***In the Rain Forest* (Pledger)
- "Animal Action I" from "Kids in Motion" (song)
- "Animal Action II" from "Kids in Motion" (song)

Week 2
- **The Very Hungry Caterpillar* (Carle)
- *Bugs! Bugs! Bugs!* (Barner) or *I Love Bugs!* (Dodd)
- *Under One Rock: Bugs, Slugs, and Other Ughs* (Fredericks, Dirubbio)
- *Heat Wave* (Spinelli)
- **Knuffle Bunny* (Willems)
- *Little Kids First Big Book of Bugs* (Hughes)
- ***Chameleon, Chameleon* (Cowley)
- ***Ten Little Ladybugs* (Gerth)
- ***It Looked Like Spilt Milk (Shaw)*
- "We're Going On a Bear Hunt" from "Kids in Action" (song)
- "Bop 'Til You Drop" from "Kids in Action" (song)

Week 3
- **Ten Black Dots* (Crews)
- *Albert* (Napoli)
- *Chrysanthemum* (Henkes) or *Sheila Rae, the Brave* (Henkes)
- *Moonbear's Shadow (Asch)*
- *Quick as a Cricket* (Wood)
- ***My Shadow* (Stevenson)
- ***Hi Fly Guy* (Arnold)
- ***Birds Build Nests* (Winer)
- "Balancing Act" from "Kids in Motion" (song)

Key
* = Book used in literacy lesson
** = Book used in extra lessons

Week 4
- **Ten Apples Up On Top* (Seuss as LeSeig)
- *Madeline* (Bemelmans)
- ***Friends at School* (Bunnett) ***Hello, School Bus* (Parker)
- ***Kindergarten ABC* (Rogers) ***Froggy Goes to School* (London)

May Focus Page

🖨 Copy on yellow paper

✂ Cut out shapes & mount on white paper

🪄 Laminate for durability

I i Y y Z z I O

BPP0511

The Block Plan Preschool, BPP0511

REFERENCES

Colorado State University Cooperative Extension. *High Altitude Baking.* 2nd ed. Ed. Patricia Kendall. Boulder, CO: 3D Press, Inc., 2005.

Common Core State Standards for English Language Arts and Literacy in History/ Social Studies, Science, and Technical Subjects. United States: Common Core State Standards Initiative, 2010. http://www.corestandards.org/wp-content/ uploads/ELA_Standards1.pdf

Common Core State Standards for Math. United States: Common Core State Standards Initiative. http://www.corestandards.org/wp-content/uploads/ Math_Standards1.pdf

Core Knowledge Foundation. *What Your Kindergartner Needs to Know: Preparing Your Child for a Lifetime of Learning.* Revised ed. Ed. E.D. Hirsch and John Holdren. New York, NY: Bantam Dell, 2013.

—. *What Your Preschooler Needs to Know: Get Ready for Kindergarten.* Ed. E.D. Hirsch and Linda Bevilacqua. New York, NY: Bantam Dell, 2008.

Core Knowledge Preschool Sequence. Canada: Core Knowledge Foundation, 2013. Pages 125-129. http://www.coreknowledge.org/mimik/mimik_uploads/ documents/494/CKFSequence_PreK_Rev.pdf

Cross, Gary. *Kids' Stuff: Toys and the Changing World of American Childhood.* Cambridge, Massachusetts: Harvard University Press, 2001.

Elkind, David. *The Hurried Child: Growing Up Too Fast Too Soon.* Cambridge, Massachusetts: Da Capo Press, 2001 and 2007.

—. *Miseducation: Preschoolers at Risk.* New York, New York: Alfred A. Knopf, Inc., 1987.

Gates, Sr., William H. Address. Ounce of Prevention Fund Luncheon. 17 Apr. 2007. http://www.gatesfoundation.org/media-center/speeches/2007/04/william-h-gates-sr-ounce-of-prevention-fund-luncheon

Gentner, Dedre. "Analogical Inference and Analogical Access." *Analogica.* Morgan Kaufmann, 1988. 63-88.

Gentner, Dedre, Ratterman, M.J., et al. "Two Forces in the Development of Relational Similarity." *Developing Cognitive Competence: New Approaches to Process Modeling.* Taylor and Francis Group, 1995. 263-313.

Ginsburg, Herbert P. and Sylvia Opper. *Piaget's Theory of Intellectual Development.* 3rd ed. Englewood Cliffs, New Jersey: Prentice Hall, 1988.

Ginsburg, Kenneth R. "The Importance of Play in Promoting Healthy Child Development and Maintaining Strong Parent-Child Bonds." *Pediatrics* 119 (2007): 182-191.

Guthrie, M.D., Elisabeth, and Kathy Matthews. *The Trouble with Perfect: How Parents Can Avoid the Overachievement Trap and Still Raise Successful Children.* New York, New York: Broadway Books, 2002.

Learning Centers (Preschool). United States: The Mailbox, 2006.

Loevinger, Jane. *Ego Development.* San Francisco, CA: Jossey-Bass Publishers, 1976.

Maxwell, Kelly L. and Richard M. Clifford. "School Readiness Assessment." *Young Children* On the Web, January 2004. http://journal.naeyc.org/btj/200401/Maxwell.pdf

Montessori, Maria. *The Montessori Method.* New York, New York: Frederick A. Stokes Company, 1912.

Pellis, Sergio, et al. The Function of Play in the Development of the Social Brain." *American Journal of Play* Vol.2 No. 3 (2010): 278-296.

Read-Aloud Roundup (Preschool). United States: The Mailbox Books, 2011.

Ritz, William. *A Head Start on Science: Encouraging a Sense of Wonder.* Arlington, Virginia: National Science Teachers Association, 2007.

Rosenthal, Robert and Lenore Jacobson. "Teachers' Expectancies: Determinants of Pupils' IQ Gains." *Psychological Reports* 19 (1966): 115-118:

Santrock, John W. *Child Development.* 11th ed. New York, NY: McGraw-Hill, 2007.

"School Readiness: A position statement of the National Association for the Education of Young Children." National Association for the Education of Young Children. Jul. 1995.

Seasonal Fun for Busy Hands (Grades PreK-K). United States: The Mailbox Books, 2008.

Selly, Patty Born. *Early Childhood Activities for a Greener Earth.* St. Paul, MN: Red Leaf Press, 2012.

Shumaker, Heather. *It's OK Not to Share...and Other Renegade Rules for Raising Competent and Compassionate Kids.* New York, New York: Penguin Group (USA) Inc., 2012.

Spiegel, Alix. "Teacher's Expectations Can Influence How Students Perform." NPR. September 17, 2012. http://www.npr.org/sections/health-shots/2012/09/18/161159263/teachers-expectations-can-influence-how-students-perform

Trister Dodge, Diane, et. al. *The Creative Curriculum for Preschool.* 4th ed. Bethesda, MD: Teaching Strategies, Inc., 2002.

ABOUT THE AUTHOR

Katy Harder is a trained, experienced early childhood professional educator with over 10 years of experience as a Pre-K curriculum developer, preschool director, preschool teacher, child care center director, kindergarten paraeducator, Pre-K sports instructor, and stay-at-home mom. A graduate of Colorado College, she wrote the Pre-K curriculum for Avid4 Adventure, the only outdoor adventure sports day camp for preschool-age children in the United States. Katy lives in Colorado with her husband and kids.

Photo by Heather Gray

THE BLOCK PLAN PRESCHOOL CURRICULUM PACK

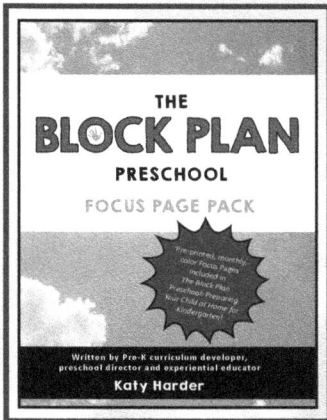

**Everything you
need to teach
your child
preschool at
home!**

Buy yours today!